PLUS ONE ON TIME

CROQUET TACTICS FOR THE MEDIUM TO HIGH HANDICAP PLAYER

D L GAUNT

*To Jill and Celia for putting up with my teaching efforts
and inspiring this book, to those who helped with comments
and advice, and to Faith for being very patient.*

Published by D L Gaunt
5 Rosedale Avenue
Stonehouse
Glos.

ISBN No. 0 9512813 0 5

Don Gaunt

The author, Don Gaunt, first started playing croquet when he discovered a set at work. With some friends, he worked out the rules and started to play. At that time he had no idea that the game was played nationally and it wasn't until he moved to Ipswich in 1979 that he played seriously. Since that time he has played in many events, both nationally and internationally. He is currently the Chairman of Ipswich and District Croquet Club, the Chairman of the East Anglia Croquet Federation and a Member of the Croquet Association Council. He holds grades 1 and 3 coaching badges and has been the organiser of coaching at Ipswich for the last 5 years. This book represents a distillation of tactical skills for beginners and improvers, based on his teaching experiences. The diligent reader will, if these tactics are learned and used correctly, see a significant improvement in his/her game.

Contents

Chapter 1

An Introduction
to the Book

*W*hy write the book? Several things prompted me. I have been coaching beginners and improvers for some years now. I thought therefore that it would be a good idea to put the results of my experience on paper. That way other coaches could benefit by having things written down for them. Also, players would have a permanent record of the points covered. My book will also help those who are not able to get regular coaching and would like to improve their tactics. The scope of my book is deliberately narrow, since books for beginners and books for experts already exist. My book will help to fill the gap.

The book will be of benefit if you have a handicap which lies between 6 and 18 inclusive. My aim is to improve your knowledge and tactical skills so that you will play well enough to have your handicap reduced eventually to below 6. I will assume that you have played for at least one season. I will also assume that you know the basic rules and strategy of the game and most of all, want to improve your play. I shall cover handicap singles and doubles, full bisque and short croquet play.

I shall not teach advanced play, or the skills of making shots (practice is probably the best teacher anyway). I will discuss some, but not all, of the rules.

The main chapters of the book (2,3 & 4) cover aspects which are common to all types of handicap game. For the convenience of the reader they cover three ranges of handicap. These are 18 to 13, 12 to 9, and 8 to 6. Each of these chapters may have a differing number of sections but all will contain advice on three situations. These are receiving bisques, giving them, and no bisques. Note that some of the main headings in the chapters are the same. Further, some of the text may appear to be repeated. There will, however, be changes designed to reflect your improving ability. Do not skip these paragraphs thinking that you have already read them.

Figure 1.1 shows the conventions and symbols used for the diagrams in this book. I explain jargon and technical terms as they occur.

Do not read all of the book at once. It has been written so that you can gradually gain tactical skills as you improve.

● If your handicap is between 18 and 13 :-

Read this chapter.

Read chapter 2 carefully.

Do not read chapters 3 or 4 yet.

Read chapters 5 to the end.

● If your handicap is between 12 and 9 :-

Read this chapter.

Read chapter 2.

Read chapter 3 carefully.

Do not read chapter 4 yet.

Read chapters 5 to the end.

● If your handicap is between 8 and 6:-

Read this chapter.

Read chapters 2 and 3.

Read chapter 4 carefully.

Read chapters 5 to the end.

Before getting down to actual play in chapter 2, I want to say a few words about your approach to a game and how to start one.

Your attitude to the game

You must approach all sports, including Croquet, in the right way. If you believe that you are going to lose, you will. If you believe that you are going to win, you might not, but your chances of doing so are much better. "Terrific," I hear you say. "We all KNOW that. How do you DO it?"

The answer is — Practice. Learn an attitude of mind, it can be done. Practice being calm, practice thinking before shooting, practice concentration on the shot in hand not the next one. When something goes wrong, practice forgetting it, or it will destroy the next shot, then the next etc. If you are naturally nervous or depressive, you can still overcome the problem, but it may take a little longer. If you want to get deeply into this subject there are books on "the inner game," try your library.

Croquet is one of the few sports left where professionalism is minimal. Even the rules of the game place a reliance on you to admit a fault. Where else would you see a player tell a referee that while observing for one error, she/he missed another? Long may this attitude exist say I, and it is up to you to keep it that way. I know that it is very tempting to pretend that the croqueted ball moved, when you know that it did not — especially if your opponent is not watching. However if you go on to win the game, victory is hollow. You know, even if your opponent does not, that you did not deserve the win. Be a good winner and a good loser (or as good as you can manage!).

You will often hear people say "the game is only over when both balls are pegged out." This seems trite but is not. Croquet is one of the few games where recovery from an apparently impossible situation not only can happen, but does, and regularly. I once saw a game in the Northern Championships. Here one player, having missed with one ball, pegged out the other. This left his opponent with only three balls on the lawn and still to score. From this position the opponent then won in two turns. This may not be a very common event but it illustrates my point, "never give up." The situation may look desperate but it will change with only one mistake by your opponent or one good hit by you. Then you have the innings and hence the initiative. Do not fall into the trap of making

9

a wild shot at an impossible hoop. Do not try a "suicide shot" at an opponent without assessing the situation first. Often, with a bit of thought, a carefully placed ball will put pressure on your opponent and force an error.

On the other side of the coin, when you are potentially in a winning situation, you really need your power of concentration. You will often hear an "out player" (the one not playing!) say "Doesn't she/he EVER make a mistake?" That player probably does make mistakes, but by concentrating on the game those mistakes reduce to a minimum. What is more, the mistakes are those of normal play and not silly careless ones.

The type of play that I will be teaching in this book is that which I have called "prudent aggression." The best way to improve is to get straight on the lawn when you know the rules and try to play constructive croquet. To help you in the early stages you will get extra turns, called bisques. As you improve, so those bisques will disappear and eventually you will be able to meet good players on equal terms. A word of warning however. Aggressive play in the early stages leads to many defeats. This is because trying to play constructive breaks involves a risk of failure. When you are a beginner, those failures come often — and all too frequently to an opponent who is not playing constructively. Do not get downhearted about it and start to play negatively, saying "Well at least I win occasionally now." In the short term this may be true. If however you persist at breakmaking your skill will improve and you will not only win occasionally but often.

Before the start

1. Make sure that you know what you are playing.

This is not as silly as it sounds. If you are in more than one event in a tournament, it is quite possible that you have mixed up the games. You may think, for example, that you are playing a full bisque event. In fact you are playing in a normal handicap game and confusion will soon reign!

2. Make sure that you know the time limits.

It is very annoying to pace yourself for a three hour time limited game only to find there are no time limits.

3. Make sure about practice.

Normally you cannot practice. If you are starting late and your opponent has played a game already that day, the manager will usually allow you a few minutes. Ask him/her first, however, before doing so.

4. Make sure that the bisque situation is correct.

Traditionally your low handicap opponent gets the bisques, puts them in the ground, then pulls them out as you spend them! This is not an absolute rule but never pull a bisque out without letting your opponent know you are doing it. An exception would be in the case of your opponent's temporary absence. In this case, say so immediately on his or her return.

Starting a game

It is worthwhile spending a minute on the options that are available to you if you win the toss. Traditionally the lower bisquer spins the coin.

i. You may choose colours. For some reason many players have a favourite pair. Avoid doing this for you are at a psychological disadvantage if you do not get "your" colours. Do however examine the balls quickly to see if one pair looks slightly better than the other. Ask if you can change any badly damaged ball. There is a lot of talk about the black ball swelling up in heat. I suppose it does a little, but not enough to worry about. It is worth noting however that for some reason which is not clear, the black ball seems to get more damage than the others, so watch out for that.

If you choose colours your opponent has choices ii and iii which follow.

If you take choice ii or iii your opponent may only choose colours.

ii. You may choose to go in first. This might seem the obvious choice since you appear to get the first innings. We shall see however, this may not always be the best thing for you to do.

iii. You may choose to go in second. I discuss in later chapters the pros and cons of doing this.

11

OK, we are ready, so on your marks and turn to chapter 2.

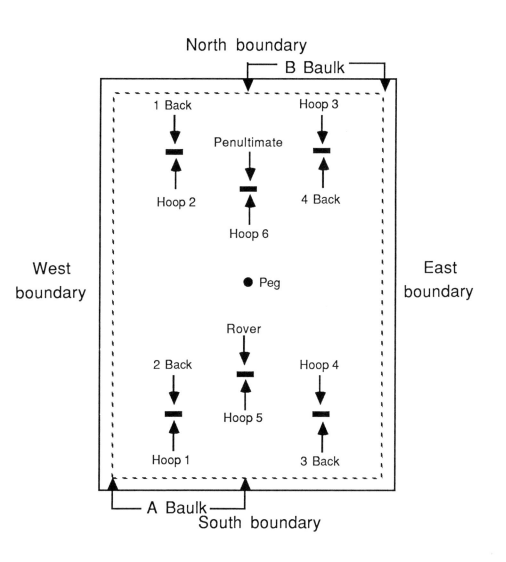

North boundary

B Baulk

1 Back

Hoop 3

Penultimate

Hoop 2

4 Back

Hoop 6

West boundary

● Peg

East boundary

Rover

2 Back

Hoop 4

Hoop 5

Hoop 1

3 Back

A Baulk

South boundary

Fig 1.1(a)   Layout of the court.

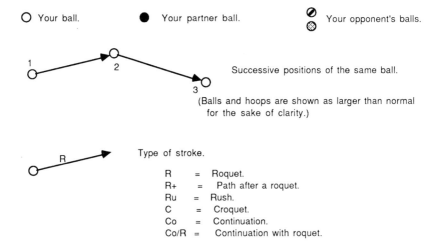

○ Your ball.   ● Your partner ball.   ⊘ Your opponent's balls.

1 ——————→ 2   Successive positions of the same ball.
○   ○
          ↘ 3 ○

(Balls and hoops are shown as larger than normal
for the sake of clarity.)

R ——————→   Type of stroke.
○
                   R   =   Roquet.
                   R+   =   Path after a roquet.
                   Ru   =   Rush.
                   C   =   Croquet.
                   Co   =   Continuation.
                   Co/R   =   Continuation with roquet.

Fig 1.1(b)   Symbols and conventions used.

14

Chapter 2

On Your Marks!

*T*o use this chapter you will have a handicap between 18 and 13 and will have had some form of introductory training. You should therefore:

● Understand the basic rules of croquet. Examples are roquets, croquets, order of hoops, pegging out.

● Understand the basic definitions of croquet. Examples are when a ball is through a hoop, off the lawn, or has made a roquet.

● Be aware of the basic faults in croquet. Examples are failing to move the croqueted ball, playing the wrong ball, crushing a ball in the hoop. You need not know the penalties in detail.

● Understand, but not necessarily do, 4 and 3 ball breaks.

If you feel unsure about any of the above points, you may have difficulties with this book. You should work on the problem before proceeding further.

Your picture of yourself

Being in this handicap range will normally mean that you have played quite a lot of games. However it will be rare for you to make breaks of more than two or three hoops without using bisques. You will only have a rudimentary knowledge of tactics, will often miss simple shots and will stick in hoops from simple approaches. This may seem like an insulting way to start a lesson! It is not, I want you to think about your capabilities in an objective way. It is important for you to do this so that you know what you can and cannot do. This is just as much a part of your overall game plan as estimating what your opponent can and cannot do.

Think of a situation.

You are in front of your hoop at an angle. You have no pioneer ball at the next hoop and you have approached this hoop off your opponent's ball. You know that you are not very good at hoop running. Yet I bet that you will still have a go! Why? Because it is human nature to take risks. You have to overcome that instinct and say to yourself "No, wait until next time."

So what do you do?

You plan to your ability. You consider the essential shots that go to make up a game. Then you fix in your mind what you can and cannot do. So:-

1. Roquets.

What is the farthest distance over which you can be pretty certain to make a roquet? If you then have a shot longer than that, cconsider the situation. You are likely to miss, what are the consequences of that miss?

2. The croquet stroke.

i. Angles. How good are you at judging them? Remember that only a couple of degrees error in your angle will give a yard of error in position over 25 yards. Know your ability to judge and don't try for positions within 6 inches when you normally cannot do better than 2 feet.

ii. Strength. There are many types of stroke from stop shot to roll and from straight shot to take off. For each there is a whole range of strengths needed to get your ball the same distance each time. Know how good you are at each type of stroke. Then combine this knowledge with (i) and you will have a circle of lawn which each ball will end up in. However you don't know where in that circle. The better you get, the smaller that circle will become.

iii. Rolls and stop shots. If you are not very good at these, try to avoid doing them until you can practice and get better. If you have to do them, and you often will, again know your limitations. If you cannot roll two balls across the width of the lawn, why try to do so in a match? Use some strategy that will enable you to play shots that will work, even if it means

16

giving up the innings. It will be better to do that and leave yourself in control rather than breaking down. If you break down, your opponent will be able to seize the advantage without effort.

3. Running hoops.

Know the maximum angle and distance from which you can be confident of scoring. A lot depends on the situation. There is much less pressure when your partner ball is the other side of the hoop and not your opponent's. Hoop running is a very psychological thing anyway. The very best players have stuck in hoops from a foot in front, just because it was a vital hoop. Somehow that hoop seems to squeeze tighter just as you take your shot. The key is calmness. Lining up, practice swings and follow through help to get the mechanics right but unless you are calm your chances are poor. Yes I know it is easy to say, and I get as nervous as anyone, but that doesn't make me wrong!

So, what does this all add up to?

It adds up to a picture that you have in your mind of your ability. It means that you can base your play on that picture in such a way that you will reduce the number of unforced errors that you make. It will mean that you can stop when you should, and not when you have to. Also you will proceed confidently when you know that you can. Of course it won't always work. Any assessment of a situation will involve the risk of failure. If you do fail, look at that failure objectively. Say for example that you have just missed a 3 yard roquet and you don't normally miss. If you have hit a dozen similar roquets successfully before this one, then forget your miss. It may have been the lawn, a lapse of concentration, or some similar one-off cause. If however you have missed three in succession, something is wrong. Until you can find out what it is, make a temporary adjustment to that picture of yourself.

Your picture of your opponent.

Ideally this should be as good as the picture you have of yourself. If you play someone regularly, it may be pretty good, but obviously will not be perfect. Whether it is a regular opponent or not, you should always watch them playing. By watching opponents you can continually update your information about them. Also it is good practice to make sure that they do not commit a fault.

What about at the start of a game?

At this stage against a new opponent you know little or nothing. You can however start with a few basic premises based on their handicap. Now I stress that what follows is only a guide, modified as play progresses. I know minus players who are very poor at hitting long shots, but once they do are almost certain to go round. Similarly I know players who can hit almost anything on the lawn, but find break constructing a hard task.

1. Minus players.

Will hit most roquets of less than 14 yards and many at any distance. Will place balls in a croquet stroke accurately to within feet on long shots and inches on short ones. Accurate through hoops but because they get good position so often can sometimes stick in awkward ones. Can pick up a four ball break from almost anything and will rarely break down from it. Have no trouble with a three ball break and can often do a two ball for several hoops. Will be tactically good and know how to put pressure on you. If you are improving and using your bisques well you will probably win. If you use your bisques poorly, you will almost certainly lose.

2. Scratch to 5 players.

Will hit most roquets less than 10 yards and many longer ones. Usually good on croquet strokes but not always. Normally they are good at hoops. Can pick up a four ball break from difficult positions, but may break down trying. Will not normally break down having got one. Will quite often break down on a three ball break. Tactically fairly good but will make errors of judgement, giving you chances. Standards of play vary a lot in this range, hence so do your chances of winning, so watch carefully!

3. Handicap 6 to 8 players.

Players in this range who are still improving will probably play much like those in 2. However they will break down more often due to lack of tactical experience and through trying shots beyond their capabilities. Since they will be like you, striving to get better, winning will need 100% effort.

Players in this range who are not improving will usually either be good at roquets or will be very poor indeed. They will be tactically unsound.

They may well play "Aunt Emma" (splitting opponent's balls far apart with no other purpose than to separate them). They will break down often, but will then suddenly produce an all-round break from nowhere. This will happen especially if you get careless and think that you have an easy victory. Play carefully and you will nearly always win.

4.   Handicap 9 to 12 players.

You will often find yourself with an advantage against improving players in this range. They will still largely be relying on bisques to get round, and against you they do not have any. See later on how to use your bisques. They will be good hitters and hoop runners. This is because they will not know enough about tactics to realise how dangerous some shots are. Hence they are relaxed and do not muff them! Tactically they will be weak and should leave you a lot of chances.

For other players the comments that I made previously hold good but the likelihood of a big break is less.

5.   Handicap 13 to 18 players.

These players are the same as you, unless you or they are wrongly handicapped, as you will be just before the handicapper spots you!

The four ball break

This is not a lesson on the mechanics of the break, as you should know those. It is a look at some of the tactics employed to maintain the break using bisques. For the moment I will assume that you have an infinite number of bisques. When a four ball break is in progress, you will have the following ball positions.

● A ball in the middle, the pivot ball.
● A ball at the next hoop after the one that you are about to run, the pioneer ball.
● A ball just past the hoop that you are about to run.
● Your ball in front of the hoop that you are about to run.

Figure 2.1, which assumes that you are at the start of a four ball break at hoop 1, illustrates this. From here the sequence is,

ON YOUR MARKS!

- Run the hoop
- Roquet the ball near the hoop
- Croquet that ball as your next pioneer, placing your ball near the pivot
- Roquet the pivot ball
- Take off to the old pioneer
- Roquet it
- Croquet the two balls to end up in the same position that you started with, only at the next hoop
- Keep going until you want to stop

I will now consider each of the elements of this sequence in turn.

- Run the hoop

Ideally you should be nicely in front, about a foot away. If you are, then going through will only require that you are careful — but BE careful!

If you are in front more than a foot away or at a slight angle, but still confident, then try for it. Don't hammer at it with all your strength. Hitting hard will destroy your aim resulting in a bounce off the hoop. Also you will almost certainly end up in a hopeless position. If you do go through, it will be with such strength that the return roquet will be a long one. Hit with enough strength to go through the hoop and land near the other ball. If you don't hit too hard and don't make the hoop, the chances are that you will stop in the jaws. Then you can run the hoop by taking a bisque.

Consider now that you have got in front but are quite a long way away. Perhaps you are also at an angle. It is time to think about taking a bisque. Remember that you still have a continuation shot before you need to take any bisques. Remember also that you do not HAVE to take a bisque, even if you have said that you will. You cannot however say that you will not take a bisque, leave the lawn, then say that you will after all! The temptation is to use your continuation shot to get into perfect position. Unless this shot is a very simple one, do not take it. It is usually far better to use the continuation shot to get a perfect rush on the other ball near your hoop. When you take the bisque you then start with a simple roquet. This will give you a much easier approach shot to the hoop. Figure 2.2 illustrates this.

How do you decide which shot to go for? You do it by referring to your picture of yourself and deciding which shot stands the best chance of succeeding. Are you good at positioning? Can you rush accurately? Can you do accurate short croquet shots? Which are you best at? Decide and make your shots accordingly (if you are bad at all of them then it's back to the practice ground!). Finally, you may have done too well and got within an inch or two of the hoop. The same points apply as above, but with the added complication that you now have a hampered shot. You must ask a referee to watch this; see the chapter on how to deal with hampered shots.

● Roquet the ball near the hoop.

The position of this ball is determined by the croquet stroke which put your ball in front of the hoop. Getting in front of the hoop is obviously the most important objective. This does not mean that the position of the other ball is unimportant. It is, because there will be two things that you will want to do when making this roquet.

1. The roquet should be an easy one. You will want to put the croqueted ball a convenient distance past the hoop and slightly to one side. What is a convenient distance? It depends very much on how hard you normally go through a hoop. Most high bisquers tend to over estimate their hoop control and do not send the croqueted ball far enough. I suggest that you try for about six feet past and see how that works, modifying the distance with experience. Slightly to one side? About 2 feet is a sensible distance.

2. You will want to rush to a good position. This position should make the creation of a new pioneer and the approach to the pivot easy. In general terms this means that you want a rush towards the peg, (where the pivot ball should be). The following table shows the position that you should try to attain for each hoop. Figure 2.3 illustrates the table.

Hoop.   Shows the hoop in question.

Distance.   Shows how far past the hoop you should send the croqueted ball.

Side.   Shows the side of the hoop that you should send the croqueted ball. This is as seen when looking at the playing side of the hoop.

Pioneer. Shows which will be the pioneer hoop when you have run this one. Thus, when you have run hoop 1, the pioneeer will be hoop 3.

Hoop	Distance	Side	Pioneer	Comments
1	6 ft	R	3	
2	4 ft	R	4	Rush back
3	6 ft	R	5	
4	4 ft	R	6	Rush back
5	6 ft	R	1B	Short shot
6	4 ft	R	2B	Rush back
1B	6 ft	L	3B	
2B	4 ft	L	4B	Rush back
3B	6 ft	L	Pen	
4B	4 ft	L	Rover	Rush back
Pen	Depends on finish wanted			
Rover	Depends on finish wanted			

Notes.

Assumes that six feet is your distance — if not adjust accordingly.

Assumes that the pivot ball is in the middle, if not adjust accordingly. (If you don't have a pivot at all, then you haven't got a four ball!)

● Croquet that ball as your next pioneer, placing your ball near the pivot

I mentioned earlier that the rush should allow you to create the pioneer easily. What do I mean by an easy shot? If you watch top players you will rarely find them making complicated rolls and splits. The only times that they will do so is to get out of trouble or when doing complex breaks involving peels. By far the easiest croquet stroke to play is the straight drive. This is where your ball and the croqueted ball both go in the same direction, and you take your shot from a normal stance with a normal swing. In this type of shot the croqueted ball goes about 4 times the distance of your ball.

So you rush to a position which is on a line from your pioneer hoop to the pivot ball and a little short. See the diagram below for an illustration.

Rush to here.   Pivot Ball   Pioneer Hoop

O   O   H

< --x Yards---- > < ------------ x Yards times four -------------- >

The balls do not have to be dead in line. In fact it is a slight nuisance if they are! As long as they are close to a line, the shot will be a simple one. All you need to concentrate on then, is the strength of shot and hitting the ball properly. As an example, Figure 2.4 illustrates the rush and pioneer shot having run hoop 1.

● Roquet the pivot ball

There is not a lot to say here. Remember not to rush it too far from the middle. If it is off centre, place your ball so that you rush back towards the middle of the lawn again.

● Take-off to the old pioneer

A lot of people worry about take-offs. There is no need to. There are several ways to line up a take-off, this is mine.

Look down at the two balls in contact (your ball on the left). Then imagine that you have a pencil and draw two circles round the balls. Where the two circles meet and touch, you can see two arrowheads. The one pointing away from you points to where your ball will go in a take-off shot. Remember that you must move or shake the croqueted ball. So make that arrowhead point to where you wish your ball to go. Figure 2.5 illustrates this technique. Then strike just to the right of this direction. If your ball is on the right hand side, you must of course hit slightly to the left. Remember that you are virtually only hitting one ball, so don't overhit it. With care you can make these shots very accurate and will be able to get good position for the last shot in this sequence.

● Croquet the two balls to end up in the same position that you started with, only at the next hoop —

and off you go again!

● Keep going until you want to stop

There will be only two reasons why you will want to stop. Either you do not want to go further or you cannot because you have reached the peg.

You will want to stop before the peg when you do not want to take the risk of your ball being pegged out. How far you go will depend on the situation. Here is a rough guide against differing opponents. This assumes that your other ball (the backward ball) has more than 6 hoops to go. ALSO you do not have enough bisques left to be reasonably certain of getting the other ball round. If you do have enough bisques left — go to peg always.

Minus players. Stop at four — back.

Scratch to 5. Stop at penult.

Handicap range 6 to 10. Stop at rover.

Handicaps over 10. Go to peg.

With less than 6 hoops to go with the backward ball, decide according to the merits of the situation.

All of the above seems to leave a risk of being pegged out. Yes it does, but it is a calculated risk and you have to take it sometimes. If you creep up hoop by hoop to the peg, you will give your opponent too many chances of a hit in. In any case as you will see in a later chapter, being pegged out is not the end of the world.

OK, so you have decided where you want to stop (before you have got there!) and you will want to plan your finish.

There are hundreds of varieties of finish. I am only going to talk about one because more would confuse, and this one is simple and effective. The leave is this, illustrated in Figure 2.6 with the assumption that you are for hoop 1 with your partner ball.

Put one of your opponent's balls at the first hoop that you want with your backward ball. Put the other either at the next hoop, or if that is too close to another ball, the next hoop but one. Put your own balls as far away as possible from the opponent's. Leave a rush for the ball which is not at your hoop but make sure that you do not leave a double. If you cannot have a rush without leaving a double, forget the rush. For picking up the break afterwards (assuming your opponent misses!) see the section on bisques.

Oh dear! It's gone wrong!

There are so many things that could go wrong that a list would be enormous. I have simplified them into two categories.

1. Errors that are a disaster.

Here things have gone so badly wrong that to recover, even using bisques, will not be worth it. It is always worth recognising fatal errors for what they are, because you may lose the innings but save the game.

Examples.

"Yo-yo bisques" or "windscreen wipers." This is where you miss a 10 ft roquet and go 10 ft past, take a bisque and miss again, etc, etc. I have seen 4 bisques used in this way, and still no roquet made. If you miss after the first bisque, give up unless you are very, very close.

The four-ball has crumbled to nothing and you only have a few bisques left. Use one bisque for a tidy finish and play the game tactic appropriate to only a few bisques (Section (b) later).

"Hoopitus." You have bounced off twice from the same hoop, or you have failed twice to approach it properly. Give up and close your turn gracefully.

2. Recoverable errors.

Recovery from a mistake will involve the taking of a bisque (or more). Remember that a bisque is an extra turn. This means that you can roquet all of the balls again. This is a very important point. Suppose that you have just failed to get in front of your hoop (with a continuation shot left, as described earlier). If you have a perfect break, then all that you need to do is use a bisque to get good position next time. Suppose though that your pivot ball has gone 10 yards away from the middle. Why not use the continuation shot to get near to the pivot ball. Then take a bisque and rush it to the middle and take off to the ball by your hoop. That way you will have restored the break and still have made the hoop. Figure 2.7 shows these moves.

This all sounds too perfect — and it is! The problem is of course that you are making five strokes before running the hoop instead of three. So weigh up the situation. What are the benefits? How difficult is what you are proposing? What will happen if it goes wrong? What will happen if you DON'T correct it, but DO get the hoop? Weigh up, make a decision and go for it. Do not start thinking about what you might have done, concentrate on executing your chosen option correctly.

As I have said, the combinations of positions are endless. Here however are a few useful do's and don'ts.

● Don't try for pickups beyond your capability. For example do not try a sequence that involves rolling two balls together for the full length of the lawn.

● Don't waste bisques "to get them out of the way because I play much better when they have gone." This is rubbish! If you do, it is because you haven't learnt to use bisques properly.

● Do use bisques as often as needed to maintain a break. I have seen players refuse to take one bisque to maintain a perfect four ball break. They then use two a few turns later to set one up again.

● Do use a half bisque properly. If used to set up a break, followed by a full bisque to continue it, then a half bisque is as powerful as a full one. On its own it is only used defensively, useful but not as effective.

Right, let us start a game.

I am still assuming that you have many bisques. If you win the toss, you should go in second. The reason for this is that you intend to get going as soon as possible. By going second you get, on the fourth turn, the first opportunity when there are four balls on the lawn. Also it prevents the very good player from having a hit in chance on fourth turn and going round.

There are many start variations and all have their pros and cons. Some guidance is needed, so here are a few ideas. Do not treat them as anything more than a first introduction on how to start. The descriptions first ball, second ball, etc refer to the order in which balls are brought into play regardless of who plays them.

I shall begin with the situation where you have lost the toss, and your opponent has put you in first.

First and third balls are yours — send the first ball near to the peg. Normally the opponent will then go for option i, ii, or iii below (see next paragraph if this does not happen). Whatever they do, put your third ball in 4th corner, or if occupied, the 2nd.

Second ball is your opponent's — i.   It will probably be sent to 2nd or 4th corner or near.

                    ii.   A short tice will be laid.

                    iii.   A long tice will be laid.

Unless remarkably brave or foolhardy your opponent will not shoot at your ball in the middle. If he/she has, you will have to decide what to do with the outcome, whatever that is. If you can make hoops without difficulty, do so. Otherwise put your opponent's ball in front of hoop 2 and lay up near 2nd or 4th corner. Remember that you may start from the A or the B baulk, whichever is most advantageous to you.

Fourth ball is your opponents — It is virtually certain that your opponent will shoot. The shot will be at a ball which if missed, leaves the fourth ball in or near a corner. If your opponent makes the roquet she/he may make a break. Whatever the situation, you will eventually get to play turn number 5. Your objective should be to get to peg and only have used half of your bisques, or less. This is aggressive croquet — the best kind — and there are some risks. The advantages both tactical and psychological are enormous though, if you get it right.

There are many combinations possible at this stage. As an example see Figure 2.8. Assume that your opponent put one ball into corner 2 and shot and missed your ball in the middle with the other. The ball then landed in the B baulk near corner 3.

So you have your balls in the middle and in corner 4, while your opponent is in corners 2 and 3. This may seem an impossible situation but it is not!

Shoot at corner 3 (not the ball) with your ball that is in corner 4. Take a bisque and rush the ball at corner 3 a few yards towards hoop 6. You should give yourself a clear view of hoop 1. Croquet the ball to hoop 1 landing with your ball near the pivot at the middle. Roquet the pivot ball and take off to the ball in corner 2. Roquet that and send it to hoop 2 with a normal drive shot. Take position near the ball at hoop 2 with the continuation stroke. Take a second bisque and simply take off via the pivot ball to your ball at hoop 1. You have a four ball break in two bisques and no difficult shots except the first, which requires some care.

When should you hold back and play a waiting game? If you are really tense, perhaps because you have just lost a previous game due to bad play on your part, then wait. If conditions (bad weather or lawn) make playing a lottery, then use bisques sparingly. Otherwise go for it!

Now assume that you have won the toss and are going in second.

First ball is your opponent's —

i.   It will probably go to or near 2nd or 4th corner. Send your second ball near to the peg.

ii.   A short tice will be laid. Put your second ball into 4th or 2nd corner whichever seems safest (4th is normally best). You may be able to do this AND have a shot at the tice. If you can, and hit, put both balls into the middle, but don't leave a double.

iii.   A long tice will be laid. Send your ball into the 4th corner.

Third ball is your opponent's — No predictions are possible. There are three likely options.

A.   A shot at the tice.
B.   A safety shot to a corner.
C.   A shot at the nearest ball.

Fourth ball is yours — The objective should again be to get to peg using no more than half of your bisques.

There is NO situation possible where you should not be able to approach hoop 1 after three bisques. Here is the most difficult. A ball in each of corners 2 and 4, and one half-way down the east or west boundaries.

As an example, consider Figures 2.9 and 2.10. Your opponent went first and laid a longish tice. You put your ball to 4 and your opponent shot at and missed the tice landing in corner 2.

Shoot at the ball in corner 2 from B baulk. If you hit, carry on; otherwise take a bisque and make the roquet. Send that ball to the middle, putting your own ball near the original tice. Roquet that ball (if you miss, see ** at the end of this paragraph). Send it just in front of hoop 1 with a straight drive. Shoot at your ball in corner 4. If you miss, take a bisque and roquet your ball in corner 4. With a strong half roll, send the forward ball to hoop 2 and your own ball to the middle. Roquet the ball in the middle, take off to hoop 1 and away you go! If you should happen to hit the ball in corner 4, straight drive the forward ball to hoop 2. Then trickle to the middle and take the second bisque.

** If you miss, take a bisque, roquet the ball gently and with a split shot send it to hoop 1. This will put your ball near the middle. Because you have taken a bisque, you can roquet the middle ball again. Do so and take off to your ball in corner 4. Roquet it and carry on as before.

If something goes wrong — see "Oh dear! It's gone wrong!".

If you do it right, and your opponent does not hit in, the second ball round is a virtual carbon copy of the first. The exception is the peg out — see the chapter "The End Game."

If you get pegged out by your opponent see the chapter "Pegged out and one ball games." By the way, unless your opponent has made it easy for you by going to peg early with one ball, forget pegging him/her out. Peeling is too difficult at your level to be worth it. If your opponent is a minus player, do not peg her/him out at all. The ball is of more use to you still on the lawn.

If you do not manage to finish before the bisques run out, see (b or c).

If your opponent does hit in on third and fifth or fourth and sixth turns and finishes, then your opponent deserves the victory.

Playing with and without bisques.

a. Lots of bisques (10 or more)

If you have 10 or more bisques then you will be playing someone who is good by your standards. It is probable, although not certain , that once your bisques have gone, you will lose unless you play very carefully indeed.

Of course nothing is certain in croquet! Aim to get both balls to peg and still have bisques left. Of course, once you can do that, it means that you are better than your handicap. You will consequently lose some of your bisques, life is so unfair! However, that is the object of the exercise. You want to become good enough to play people on level terms and still beat them.

b.   Some bisques (9 or less).

i.   If you have a reasonable handful of bisques (5 or more) take one ball round with them. You may get a good break and still have some left. Go as far as shown in ●   Keep going until you stop. It will however pay you to wait a while for a suitable opportunity to get going with the four ball break. You cannot afford to use three or four bisques to get going as in (a).

ii.   When you only have one or two bisques to start with, or remaining, use them at the appropriate time(s). By this I mean be ever watchful for the situation where your turn plus one bisque will give you a perfect break.

As an example, Figure 2.11; You are for 1 back (with say, yellow) and 4 back. Your opponent has a four-ball but blobs hoop 4 when using your yellow leaving you an easy roquet. Using yellow make the roquet. Send that ball as a pioneer to 2 back, landing near the ball at 5. Roquet that ball, and put it to the middle. Attempt to get a rush to 1 back using the ball already in the middle (your opponent's old pivot ball). If you get it right, well done. If you do not, roll up to 1 back, take a bisque and you have a four ball.

Do not hang on to bisques too long just as a reserve. Bisques used in this way are rarely spent well. However the effect of a couple of bisques still standing is sometimes devastating to an otherwise aggressive player. They will in any case force most players to be more careful. So if you think that they are of more value standing than spent, leave them as pressure on your opponent. Not too long though or you may find yourself beaten with the bisques still there (going to bed with bisques). How embarrassing that will be!

iii.   I have said little about defensive bisques. These are used sparingly and only to get out of really serious trouble. You might wish to prevent a perfect four ball break for your opponent. You will want to save a certain loss of the game. Do use a defensive bisque if appropriate. I do not subscribe to the theory that bisques are only used for attack.

c.   You have no Bisques.

i.   If you had some and have used them, then you must now play very carefully. I do not mean play "Aunt Emma." I mean —

● Don't take chances unless there is little choice (such as your opponent being bound to finish anyway). There is a rule here — If your opponent will PROBABLY finish but it is not certain, join up. If your opponent is CERTAIN to finish barring a miracle, then take the shortest shot on the lawn.

● Don't leave doubles.

● Don't just join up for the sake of something to do. Often this will give your opponent a break that he/she had not got before.

● Wherever possible, join up near a boundary. If your opponent shoots and misses it will be easy to pick up her/his ball.

ii.   If you had no bisques to start with, then you are playing someone who has the same handicap as yourself. Unless you or they are wrongly handicapped your skill levels are similar so you will have to concentrate just that bit harder. Do not fall into the trap of relying on your opponent to make the mistakes. Remember that you will be making them as well so the advantages are cancelled out. Essentially you should behave as in (i) above except that you may well be able to take calculated risks. The basis for this is that even if you do give your opponent the innings he/she will not make much from it.

   Remember the pictures of yourself and your opponent, and build them up as the game progresses. Base your play on these pictures because they represent the true situation. Play to your real ability, not what you would like it to be! By this I mean don't try for complicated break building which is beyond your capability. Just because you can do beautiful four ball breaks with bisques does not mean that you can do them without. If you can — terrific, you're on your way down! To be realistic, at your level, the four ball break without bisques is more often obtained by accident than design. This does not mean that you should not seize the chance when it occurs, but you must be pragmatic. In this style of game you will normally be looking for breaks of one to three hoops with a safe layup at the end. Here are a few practical tips.

● What if a shot involves a long split roll to maintain a break and you cannot do long split rolls? Do a take-off instead and accept the possible end of the break. If you do this, think about how you are going to finish and still retain the advantage.

● If you cannot do long take-offs from the corner without sending the croqueted ball off lawn, don't do them! Practice them until you can, but not in the game.

● Remember the wiring law. If you do not know what it is, ask a referee to explain it to you before you start to play.

● If making a hoop is very difficult, do not try, but set up a leave as described in the section on breaks.

● If you have not got the innings and do not look much like getting it, concentrate on making it difficult for your opponent to make a break. You might put one ball in a corner. Alternatively, lurk on the boundary near, but not too near, a hoop that she/he wants to make.

iii. Be aware that your tactics when you have bisques are very different from those when you do not. This applies in situations (i & ii) above and in (d) below. I stress this point strongly. It is only the high bisquer, whose knowledge of tactics is (by virtue of being a high bisquer) imperfect who has this problem. He/she has to be able to make the switches from having many bisques — to a few — to none. I have heard many beginners say "It's like playing different games" and in a sense that is true. Only in a sense though, because it IS the same game. Unless you get ready to change your play according to the situation, you can get into trouble from what seemed an easy situation. At the time of writing my handicap is ½. I have won handicap games where my opponent has got to peg and penult (or similar) while I have not yet started. One reason why I was able to do so was because my opponents had had it easy with bisques. They had done well, but forgot that when the bisques were gone, carelessness gets punished severely by A class players.

d. Giving bisques.

The maximum number of bisques that you can give is 5, so your opponent will only be in category (b ii). Your tactical play will therefore be essentially the same as for (c). Remember to try not to give your opponent the opportunity to pick up an easy break. The most obvious pitfall to avoid is joining up near your opponent's hoop.

What else?

At this stage, nothing else. Remember this is just the start of tactics and that you at the start of the handicap range. I do not believe in teaching too much at the beginning, because to do so will only confuse. So, concentrate on getting these first tactics correct. In a very short time the handicappers attention will be drawn to you — usually by your beaten opponents! You will then be ready for the next chapter.

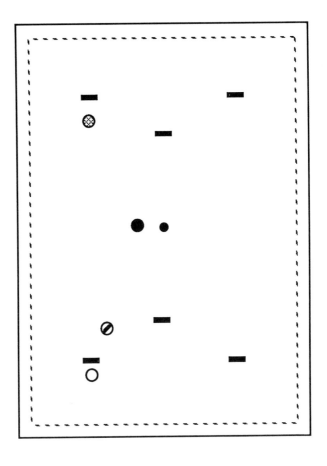

Figure 2.1   The start of a four ball break.

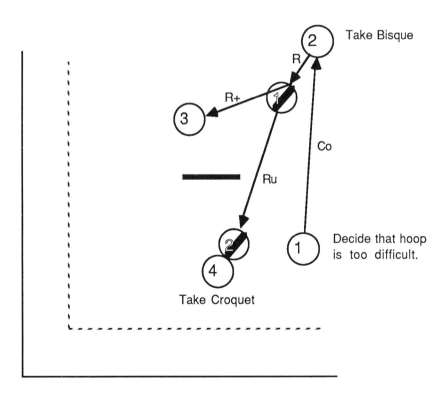

Figure 2.2   Taking a bisque having failed to approach your hoop.

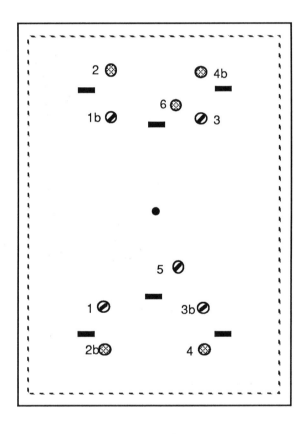

Figure 2.3   Position of the croqueted ball just prior to the running of each hoop (assumes starting position of Fig 2.1).

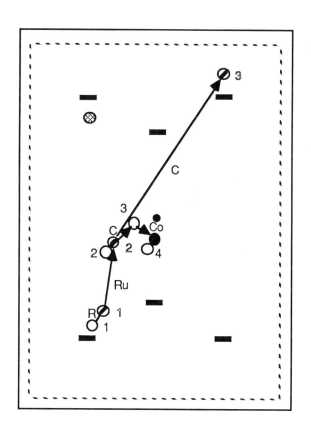

Fig 2.4   Rush and pioneer set up, having just run hoop 1.

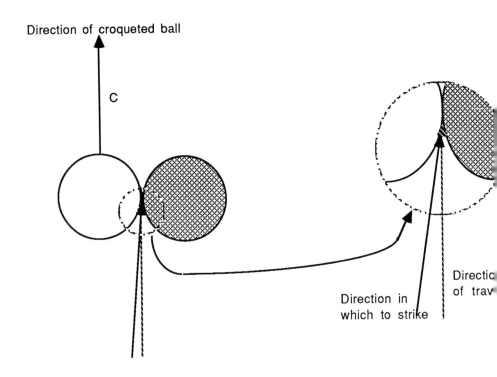

Direction of croqueted ball

C

Direction in
which to strike

Directio
of trav

Fig 2.5   The take-off.

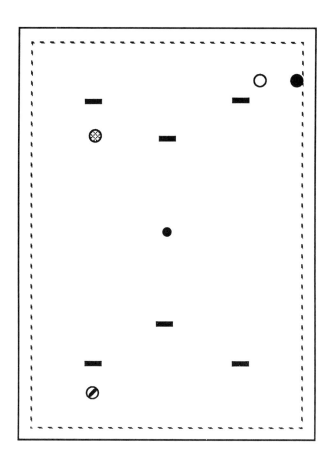

Fig 2.6   The finish after the first ball is round.

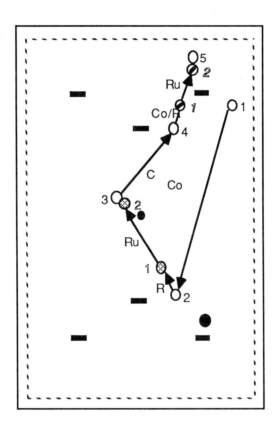

Fig 2.7   Tidying up a four ball break (assume that you are for hoop 3).

Initial position

Position just before
taking 2nd bisque

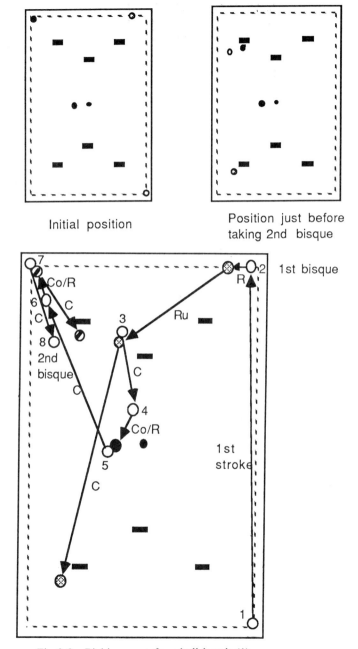

Fig 2.8   Picking up a four ball break (1).

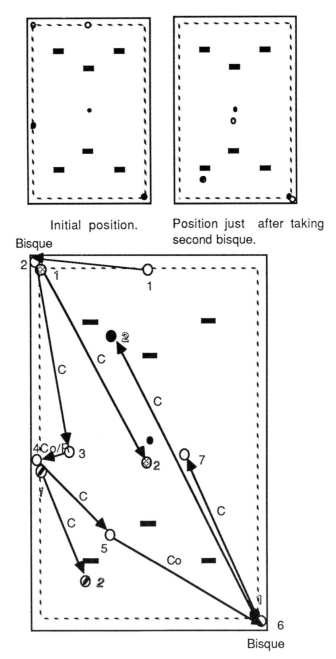

Initial position.

Position just after taking second bisque.

Fig 2.9   Picking up a four ball break (ii).

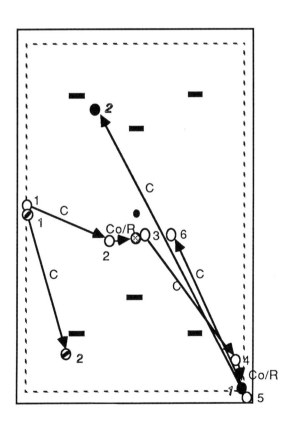

Fig 2.10   Situation (ii) if roquet on fails.

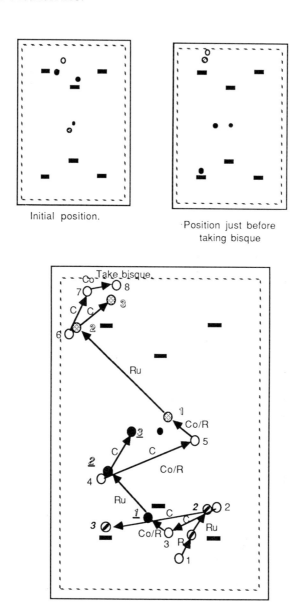

Initial position.

Position just before
taking bisque

Fig 2.11   Picking up a four ball break (iii).

Chapter 3

Get Set!

*T*o use this chapter you will have a handicap between 12 and 9. You should therefore:

● Understand the major rules of croquet. Examples are roquets, croquets, order of hoops, pegging out, peeling, rushing, doubles, full bisque and short croquet play.

● Know how to start and finish a game, including timed games.

● Understand the major definitions of croquet. Examples are when a ball is through a hoop, off the lawn, has made a roquet, is wired, is in hand, and is not replaced in the yard line.

● Know about the basic problems in croquet. Examples are failing to move the croqueted ball, playing the wrong ball, crushing a ball in the hoop, taking bisques wrongly, misplacing clips. Know the penalties in straightforward problem situations.

● Know when to call a referee.

● Understand, and put into practice, the information contained in chapter 2.

If you feel unsure about any of the above points, you should study or practice as appropriate before proceeding further.

Your picture of yourself.

By now you should be aware of the importance of attitude and approach to the game. You should have a good idea of your own capabilities and weaknesses. If you do not, then I suggest that you re-read chapters 1 & 2 carefully.

You will have played quite a number of games. Probably they were mostly in your own club. If you haven't already done so, you should now be considering some competitive croquet at other clubs. Apart from being good fun and good company, it will enable you to play different people. This will widen your experience of playing styles. Most clubs take part in local league play of some sort. There is a wide range of national events held throughout the season under the auspices of the Croquet Association (CA). You should consider joining the CA now. You will be supporting your sport. Also you will glean a wealth of information from the magazine and through CA sponsored events such as coaching weekends. Contact your Secretary for details.

In this handicap range you will be able to pick up a four ball break with one or two bisques. You will also now be starting to make breaks of several hoops without bisques. You will have a basic knowledge of tactics. Because of the confidence that you have gained by using your bisques properly, your shooting and hoop running will have improved considerably. "Oh no they haven't," I hear you mutter! They almost certainly have but your expectations have gone up as well. Good, because this means that you are ever striving to become a better player. You will still make errors of judgement, some of which will be due to an over estimation of your ability. Many though will be due to a simple lack of thought and planning. In fact planning is the theme of this chapter.

Think of a situation.

You are for 1 back with a rather untidy four ball which has the pioneer in good position but the pivot well off centre. You mess up the approach to the hoop. "That's OK" you think, take a bisque and make the hoop, which you do. However the break is untidy. This means that your positioning of the ball which goes beyond 1 back is important. This is because it is the ball that you intend to rush to a good recovery position having run the hoop. You hadn't thought of that! Now the pioneer to 3 back is difficult. You just manage it but leave yourself a long way from the poorly positioned pivot. To roquet it you go firmly — and miss.

So there you are, suddenly from a commanding position to a disaster. Why? Lack of planning. You had a continuation shot left before you took the bisque. That shot could easily have been to near the pivot ball with a rush to the middle. A simple take off shot from there to the ball at one back and the four ball is back again.

The fundamental message from this is, plan EVERY shot. I have capitalised "every" because that is exactly what I mean. If you need further convincing of this, go and watch top players in a four ball break. These players can do such a break with their eyes shut. They can easily recover from poor placing. That is not what happens. They play every stroke with care, every shot lined up and every position considered. Why? Because the discipline of a tight and careful break is part of what makes a good player good. A sloppy break player is a player who will make mistakes and mistakes cost games. You will often hear a sigh of exasperation from an A class player when a rush goes 2 feet to the side of a hoop and not in front. You think "I would have been happy with that." This is partly why you are not yet an A class player!

You might think at this stage "What has this got to do with my picture of myself?" If you remember chapter 2, I said "You plan to your ability." Well, now that you know your ability, you must plan to it. It is no use knowing your skills if you do not use them properly.

Your picture of your opponent.

You have now added planning to your own picture. You should also add your opponent's planning and tactics to your picture of him/her. Does your opponent use bisques wisely/well? Does she/he make suicide shots and hit/miss them? Are obvious break situations ignored/taken? Does your opponent refuse fairly easy hoops/roquets? Can he/she run impossible hoops or roll round on two ball breaks? Watch for these things and use the information for your own plan.

The three ball break.

There are three main reasons why you will be doing a three ball break.

i.   You have bisques, but tactically it is better to make one or two hoops on a three ball before picking up the odd ball.

ii.   You have no bisques and the odd ball is in a very difficult position to pick up.

iii.   You are pegged out. You may or may not have bisques.

Let us first of all consider the mechanics of a three ball break. In operation correctly it is simpler than a four ball. You have a pioneer and a ball at your next hoop, but no pivot. When you have run a hoop you make the next roquet. The subsequent croquet stroke has not only got to create a new pioneer, it has got to get your ball to the ball at the next hoop. The trick is to make that croquet stroke as simple as possible. To achieve THAT needs accurate placing of the ball past the hoop that you are about to run plus accurate hoop running.

When a three ball break is in progress, you will have the following. A ball at your next hoop and a ball beyond the hoop that you are running. Your ball will be in front of its hoop. From here the sequence is,

● Run the hoop

● Roquet the ball near the hoop

● Croquet that ball as your next pioneer, placing your ball near the old pioneer

● Roquet it

● Croquet the two balls to end up into the same position as the one that you started with, only at the next hoop

● Keep going until you want to stop

I will now consider each of the elements of this sequence in turn.

● Run the hoop

You should have a fairly good idea of running hoops but will probably still have some problems with control. Do not worry too much about that at this stage. What you should know, is how far you go through a hoop when you run it with your normal strength. I mentioned this aspect in chapter 2 and gave a nominal six feet. For a three ball break, accuracy is important, so you should modify the nominal figure to suit your play.

● Roquet the ball near the hoop. and
● Croquet that ball as your next pioneer, placing your ball near the old pioneer

The same croquet stroke which put your ball in front of its hoop determines the position of the ball beyond the hoop. Although getting in front of the hoop is the most important objective, the position of the other ball is also significant. It is important because you will want to rush to a position which makes it easy to create a new pioneer. At the same time you want an easy approach to the old pioneer. In general terms, this means that you want a rush to a position which gives you a straight drive stroke. It is the same as in a four ball break, see chapter 2. This time you are not rushing to the middle but to various parts of the lawn. The following table shows where you should place the ball for each hoop in turn. The positions and rush points are also illustrated in Figure 3.1.

Hoop   =   The hoop that you wish to run.

Distance   =   The distance past your hoop that you should send the croqueted ball in the hoop approach shot.

Side   =   The side of the hoop that you should place the croqueted ball (about 2 feet to the side).

Pioneer   =   The hoop to send a ball to as the pioneer, having run "Hoop."

Point to   =   The ideal rush position to give you a straight croquet rush to shot creating a new pioneer and approaching your next hoop.

*   =   Type of shot to play if Point to rush to goes wrong.

Hoop	Distance	Side	Pioneer	Point to rush to	*
1	8 ft	L	3	W boundary level with hoop 2	**
2	6 ft	R	4	N Boundary in front of hoop 3	***
3	8 ft	L	5	Between hoop 4 and E boundary	*** *
4	6 ft	R	6	Between hoop 5 and S boundary	***
5	6 ft	R	1B	Just past the peg	*** **
6	6 ft	L	2B	N boundary in front of 1 back	*** ***
1B	8 ft	R	3B	W boundary level with 2 back	***
2B	6 ft	L	4B	S boundary in front of 3 back	**
3B	8 ft	R	Pen	Between 4 back and E boundary	****
4B	6 ft	L	Rover	Between pen and N boundary.	***
Pen	6 ft	L or R	Peg	Level with peg	*** *** *
Rover	4 ft	L or R	-	Near pioneer at peg.	*** *** *

* = Shot needed from the hoop if you fail to get a rush to anywhere useful.

** = Strong split three quarter roll.

*** = Split drive.

*** * = Medium full roll.

*** ** = Half roll.

*** *** = Split stop.

*** *** * = Take off.

GET SET!

Notes.

Assumes that six feet is your distance — if not adjust accordingly.

Penultimate and rover show the situation with you pegged out with your other ball and going for a finish.

● Croquet the two balls to end up into the same position as the one that you started with, only at the next hoop

and off you go again!

● Keep going until you want to stop

If you have had one ball pegged out, you will not want to stop until you have won. Otherwise you should have managed to pick up the other ball (see next paragraph) and have a standard four ball break. If you have not picked up the other ball, you must decide how much that matters. Usually you should be able to dig it out before the end and put it somewhere useful. If that looks too difficult, or could mean loss of break control, forget it and place the other balls accordingly.

Picking up the fourth ball.

If you have many bisques, I do not advise making more than one hoop on a three ball before digging out the other ball. Only do so then if the first hoop is trivial. If not, you should wait for an opportune moment to pick up the ball. Here are a few basic ways of digging the ball out of corners (or near). All assume an accurate three ball break set up already. Usually you will need a small amount of tidying up of the four ball after you have run your next hoop. Figures 3.2.1.i to 3.2.4.iii illustrate the moves.

Corner 1.

i.   After running hoop 4, rush to near 2 back. Take off for corner one, roquet, split to hoop 6 and approach hoop 5.

ii.   After running 1 back, rush to near rover. Take off to corner 1, split to 3 back and approach 2 back.

2. Corner 2.

i.   After running hoop 1, rush to near hoop 5. Take off to corner 2, split to hoop 3 and approach hoop 2.

ii.   After running hoop 6, roquet and take off to corner 2. Roquet the corner ball and stop shot to 2 back approaching 1 back.

iii.   After running 4 back, rush to near 1 back. Take off for corner 2, roquet, split to rover and approach penult.

3. Corner 3.

i.   After running hoop 2, rush to near hoop 6. Take off for corner 3, roquet and stop shot to hoop 4, approaching hoop 3.

ii.   After running hoop 5, rush to beyond hoop 6. Take off for corner 3, roquet and half roll to 1 back, approaching 6 (not very easy this one).

iii.   After running 4 back, roquet and take off for corner 3. Roquet the corner ball, split to rover and approach penult.

4. Corner 4.

i.   After running 3, rush to near hoop 5. Take off to corner 4, roquet and half roll to hoop 5 (or to the middle if you already have a ball at 5), approaching hoop 4.

ii.   After running 4, rush back halfway to peg. Take off to corner 4, roquet and quarter roll to 6, approaching 5.

iii.   After running 2 back, rush to near rover. Take off to corner 4, roquet and drive to 4 back, approaching 3 back.

These are the easier pick-ups. More complex ones exist but have a much higher risk of breakdown. I have gone for the options which involve a medium length rush that does not need too much accuracy. This is followed by a fairly short take-off to the corner. This I feel is the safest option to start with. As your rushing and take off accuracy improve you can try for better position with the rushed ball.

These pick-ups were described without the use of bisques. You should eventually be able to accomplish them in that way. Often, however, you will have bisques. You must then decide whether you want to go for the pickup as described, or plan to spend a bisque and make the pick-up easy. For example, illustrated in Figure 3.3, situation number (i) when the ball is in corner 4 could be played as follows,

After running hoop 3, rush to the middle. Take off to the ball at 4 and roquet it gently (adjusting its position to a perfect one in front of the hoop if needed). Take off to corner 4 and roquet the corner ball. Send it to hoop 5, approaching hoop 4, take perfect position with the continuation stroke. Take a bisque and carry on with the four ball.

This play is much easier, but has cost a bisque. The play also serves as another reminder of the keyword for this chapter, planning. You have got to decide before running hoop 3 what you are going to do at hoop 4. Why? Because you will be putting the ball that is just beyond hoop 3, in the following positions.

6 ft past and on the right for taking a bisque.
8 ft past and on the right for a pick-up without a bisque.
8 ft past and on the left for a three ball break without a pick-up.

Figure 3.4 illustrates the three positions.

Oh dear! It's gone wrong!

1. Fatal errors.

Here things have gone so badly wrong that to recover, even using bisques will not be worth it. It is always worth recognising fatal errors for what they are, because you may lose the innings but not the game. This paragraph is a repeat of that in chapter 2 simply because the message bears repeating. Your skill at recovery will have improved, but so should your skill at recognising impossible situations.

2. Recoverable errors.

Here again, you will employ your improvements in shot making and tactics to aid recovery. Sounds like a patent medicine doesn't it? Well in a way it is. When you are very ill you need a lot of medicine to get better and less as you improve. In the same way you will need less bisques to recover from problems. In the last chapter I stressed that a bisque was a complete extra turn and that this fact is often used. Used not only to recover from an error, but to tidy up a loose break. This is also true when the error is one involving the rules. For example, if you fail to move the croqueted ball in a take off shot, replace the balls and your turn ends. That does not mean that you have to leave the court. You may take a bisque and start again. Because it is a new turn, you can roquet all of the balls again. This is worth remembering because it may well change your play.

Example.

You are for hoop 5. There is a ball at hoop 5 which you have not roqueted yet. A ball is near hoop 4 which you have already roqueted and a ball is in corner 4 that you have just roqueted. You are taking off from corner 4 to hoop 6. The reason for this is that you do not fancy the split shot which would send the ball in corner 4 to hoop 6 while approaching hoop 5. You fail to shake the croqueted ball and replace your ball. You take a bisque. Do not repeat the take off shot. Send the corner ball to hoop 6 with a straight drive. Next use the ball at hoop 4, sending it as a pivot and away you go with a four ball. I am assuming here that you have not got many bisques to play with — if you have, what are you doing in this mess anyway!

Playing with and without bisques

a.   Lots of bisques (10 or more)

If you have 10 or more bisques then you will be playing someone who is good, probably a minus player. Once your bisques have gone, you will need to play very carefully to avoid defeat. Look towards getting both balls to peg and still having bisques left in the same way that you did when you were a beginner. The difference will be that you are now a much better player and need less bisques to go round. If you are an improving player, you should win most games against A class players. The thing that will lose most matches of this type for you is carelessness. It all seems so easy — and essentially it is. So you make loose shots and take unnecessary risks. All of a sudden there you are, for peg and four back watching your opponent win in two turns. So concentrate, and beat your opponent by 26. Enjoy it while you can because you won't have to do it many times before the handicapper catches up with you.

In the last chapter I gave some basic advice on starting a game with many bisques. This advice still holds but you should also have worked out some variations for yourself.

As with any tactic, there is usually a counter tactic. I am going to discuss next what good players will do to extract the maximum amount of bisques from you. You will need to recognise the tactics and perhaps do something about them. Another time, when you are giving bisques to a beginner, you can use the tactics yourself.

1.   Opponent goes in first and lays a very short tice.

You have to go for it unless you cannot do so without giving a break away if you miss. If you are not happy about shooting, put your ball into corner 2 or 4 as seems appropriate (4 is normally the better choice). If you hit, then try one of these three choices.

a.   Roll both balls to the middle.

b.   Put one ball near hoop 2 and the other in the middle.

c.   Put one ball along the east boundary close to corner 3 and the other in corner 1. This last tactic is effective but tricky to execute. The problem for your opponent is getting both balls out of the corner. If she/he doesn't, you have an easy roquet and the saving of a bisque.

2.   You go first and go into corner 4. Your opponent shoots deliberately to miss but also to go into the corner. He/she then replaces his/her ball to give a double.

This one is tricky. If you go for the double, you must at least be ready to take a bisque if you miss. A lot depends on the way the balls end up. You should be able to end your turn with one ball somewhere near the middle and the other two near corner 4. Separate the two balls in the corner by enough distance so as not to leave a double target. Remember that it doesn't matter in this case if you lay up near your opponent's ball. The fourth ball must be brought into play. The risk that you take is that if your opponent hits in she/he will probably go round. Well it is your decision!

If you do not fancy the above tactic, play safe and put your second ball into corner 2. However your opponent still has that double and could well go round even though the situation is not promising.

There are other variants of your opponent shooting for or near the first ball but the approach is much the same.

3.   Your opponent goes first and shoots (and sometimes gets) hoop 1.

This is just an attempt to intimidate you! Ignore it and treat the final position of your opponent's ball on its merits.

4.   During the game your opponent leaves "tempters." These are ball positions that look as though it would be possible (but not easy) for you to set up a four ball break. Alternately, it looks likely (but not certain) that your opponent will have a good break next time if you do not hit in or take a bisque.

This is where you draw on your picture of your own or your opponent's abilities. You must balance the risks against the gains or losses and decide accordingly. There is NO absolute answer. It is said that any shot which works is the right shot. I have said it and so can you after a lucky fluke. However, if you do not mean it as a joke, you should start this book from the beginning again.

5.   Your opponent joins up, usually wide.

This is a dangerous thing for your opponent to do. It is dangerous for you if you ignore it, so don't. It is also dangerous for your opponent as it almost certainly makes it easy for you to set up a break.

If something goes wrong — see "Oh dear! It's gone wrong!".

If you do it right, and your opponent does not hit in, the second ball round is a virtual carbon copy of the first. The exception is the peg out — see the chapter "The End Game."

If you get pegged out by your opponent, again see "The End Game." By the way, unless your opponent has made it easy for you by going to peg early with one ball, forget pegging him/her out. Peeling is too difficult at your level to be worth it. If you are against a minus player, do not peg her/him out at all. The ball is more use to you still on the lawn.

If you do not manage to finish before the bisques run out, see (b or c).

b.   Some bisques (9 or less).

There is very little to add to the advice given in the previous chapter under this heading. For your convenience I have repeated it here with minor alterations, as appropriate. The players who are giving you these bisques will be better than before, but so will you be.

b i.   If you have a reasonable handful of bisques (5 or more), then get one ball round with them. You may get a good break and still have some left. Go as far as indicated in ● Keep going until you stop ● above. It will, however, pay you to wait a while for a suitable opportunity to get going with the four ball break. You cannot afford to use three or four bisques to get going as in (a). Remember that your opponent has to start sometime so you can sit tight until he/she tries. This should give you an easier break to set up. There are three basic approaches to this tactic.

A.   Put one of your balls halfway along North boundary and the other in corner 2 or 3. Then shoot from corner to corner at the middle ball. If you hit, get going. If your opponent breaks down in the middle, shoot for the corner and take bisques as needed. If your opponent goes round, pick up from the end of the break and go round yourself.

B.   Shoot at a ball, so that if you miss it you will end up a considerable distance away from it and any other ball. Keep this up as in A.

C.   With your opponent joined up do not join up yourself and then not take a bisque. The only times that I would recommend it are as follows.

C1.   To force an error from a weak opponent.

C2.   When it is difficult to get to you and difficult to make anything from you.

C3.   During the end game, see the chapter on this.

C4.   When lawn conditions are very difficult and normal play is virtually impossible.

C5.   When your opponent tries the same tactics. Then you might risk a wide join up after he/she has missed a few.

b ii.   When you only have one or two bisques to start with or remaining, use them at the appropriate time(s). By this I mean be ever watchful for the situation where your turn plus one bisque will give you a perfect break.

Do not hang on to bisques too long just as a reserve. Bisques used in this way are rarely spent well. However, the effect of a couple of bisques still standing is sometimes devastating to an otherwise aggressive player. They will in any case force most players to be more careful. So if you think that they are of more value standing than spent, leave them as pressure on your opponent. Do not leave them too long. You may find yourself beaten with the bisques still there (going to bed with bisques) and how embarrassing that would be!

iii.   I have said little about defensive bisques. These are used sparingly and only to get out of really serious trouble. Examples are a perfect four ball break for your opponent, or to save a certain loss of the game. Do use a defensive bisque when it is appropriate. I do not subscribe to the theory that bisques are only used for attack.

iv.   You will now start to get into the situation where you will have a half bisque left for very good reasons. Perhaps that is all you had to start with. Perhaps your breaks started with whole bisques because you were certain of scoring a hoop off the first bisque. In this case your main use is defence, so where do you use it, and when? My view, which some would challenge, is that you save it for an emergency. This means that you may never use it. By emergency I mean a situation which has a very high probability of leading to a match loss. One very good time to use it is when your opponent has got one ball round and has set up an ideal situation to get the other one after it. Do not use it when you are playing badly and have lost the innings half a dozen times, just to get the innings back again. Do use it at the end when you are for peg and peg but cannot get a good finish position.

GET SET!

c. i. No Bisques.

Once again, for convenience I repeat the advice given in the last chapter, with some modifications.

i. If you had some and have used them, then you must now play very carefully. I do not mean play "Aunt Emma." I mean —

● Don't take chances unless there is little choice (such as your opponent being bound to finish anyway). There is a rule here — If your opponent will PROBABLY finish but it is not certain then join up. If your opponent is CERTAIN to finish barring a miracle, then take the shortest shot on the lawn. On other occasions you need to assess the risks. Here are a few common situations that might help you to get an idea about assessing risk. Once again do not take these examples as absolute answers to problems but indicators to the best chance of success.

A. You do not have the innings.

If you do not look like getting the innings this time, concentrate on making things difficult for your opponent. Put one ball in a corner. Lurk on the boundary near, but not too near, a hoop that she/he wants to make.

Can you "shoot through?" That is, can you take a shot at a ball somewhere in the middle, landing on the boundary well away from your opponent if you miss? If so, then you have a safe shot.

Is a wide join safe? See earlier in this chapter for comments on joining up.

Do you have a double to shoot at? Doubles come in many widths. They can be the "perfect" double which is two balls separated by just under the width of one ball. At the other end of the scale you may have something which is little better than a single ball. Remember that the balls do not have to be side by side to give a double. It is the position from which you view them which counts. In the examples below X is your ball and O,O are the others.

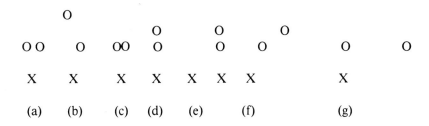

(a) Has a perfect double with effectively a triple width ball to aim at. This means that you can roughly double (not triple) the distance over which you can shoot with confidence.

(b) Also has a perfect double but because the target balls are some distance apart it is possible that the lawn may give strange results. You could miss the near ball on the right and the far one on the left. The answer is a firm shot to keep your ball on line, but not too hard or you will lose accuracy.

(c) Here the double has an effective width of two balls. The extra distance that you can add for accuracy here is only 50%. Suppose that your maximum accurate roqueting distance on a single ball is 6 yards. Your maximum accurate distance here will be 9 yards.

(d) This is not a double normally, but on a dodgy lawn it might be if you shot gently.

(e) Here you have about a ball and a quarter. Treat it as a single ball.

(f) Because of the angle, this shot gives approximately a two ball width.

(g) Now this is a different situation altogether. If the gap between the target balls is wide, you do not have a double so do not treat it as one. What about when the gap is about two balls width? It is up to you. If you are a good shot, shooting for the middle will probably mean that you will get it and miss both balls. If you are not a particularly good shot, then aim for the middle and trust to chance. Do not shoot if you are risking too much. Remember that over a distance of more than say 20 yards, the odds are against a hit. I have more to say on the subject of doubles in the next chapter.

Don't just join up for the sake of something to do. Often this will give your opponent a break that he/she had not got before.

B.   You do have the innings.

Don't leave doubles yourself.

Wherever possible, when you are finishing a turn under control, join up near a boundary. If your opponent shoots and misses it will be easy to pick up her/his ball.

Assess risks with the knowledge that you have no "get out" if you go wrong. Remember there are no bisques.

Place the balls at the end of each turn such that it is difficult for your opponent to hit in safely, and little to go on even if he/she does. Now those two requirements are not easy to meet at the same time. Having set up for a break yourself often means that it is good for your opponent as well. The only thing that you can do apart from those things already mentioned is to minimise the risk. Also do not leave loose balls in helpful positions for your opponent.

Guard the boundary. You will often finish a turn wanting to have a short rush to your next hoop. You will not want to leave a free shot through you to the boundary. The answer is a join up about 3 yards in from the boundary (2 yards from the yard line). This gives the following advantages.

● It is easier to get the rush.
● It is easier to hide behind a hoop.
● It is easy to pick up a ball from the boundary if your opponent shoots and misses.

It is easier to do something with that ball if you do pick it up (because your other ball is a few yards in, not on the boundary).

c   ii.   If you had no bisques to start with, you are playing someone with the same handicap as yourself. It means that unless you or they are wrongly handicapped your skill levels are similar. You will have to concentrate just that bit harder. Do not fall into the trap of relying on your opponent to make the mistakes. You will be making them as well so the advantages cancel out. Essentially you should behave the same as in the previous paragraph. Remember the pictures of yourself and your opponent, and build them up as the game progresses. These pictures represent the true situation. Base your play on them. Play how you are, not how you would like to be! By this I mean don't try for complicated break building which is beyond your capability. This does not mean that you should not seize the chance when it occurs, but you must be pragmatic. In this style of game you will normally expecting breaks of three to six hoops with a safe layup at the end. Here are a few practical tips.

● If a shot involves a long split roll to maintain a break and you cannot do long split rolls, do a take-off instead and accept the end of the break.

● If you cannot do long take-offs from the corner without sending the croqueted ball off lawn, don't do them! Practice them however until you can.

● Remember the wiring law. If you do not know it, ask a referee to explain it to you before you start to play.

● If making a hoop is very difficult, do not try but set up a leave as described in the section on breaks.

d.   Giving bisques.

The maximum number of bisques that you can concede is 9, so your opponent will be playing in situation (c). Unless you already know your opponent you must assume that she/he knows how to use bisques well. This means that you must avoid as far as possible making it easy for your opponent to go round. However, you cannot just lurk in opposite corners all the time, so what should you do?

You can keep the number of balls in the centre of the lawn to a minimum. This usually means getting a rush to your hoop and making it. You then either go to the next hoop on a two ball, or retire to the boundary. This approach is not much use for getting balls round. It is very useful when you are for the same hoop as your opponent. It means that you can approach the next hoop with less worry about breaking down at it. You can also start to think more constructively about a break.

If you plan to make up a break as you progress round, proceed with caution. This is tricky, requires a great deal of planning and skill, but is very rewarding. To have "picked up a break from nothing" is a most satisfying thing to do in croquet.

You can take a risk. If your opponent knows how to use bisques, then he/she is going to build up a break fairly soon anyway. It can often be a good idea to go for a shot that would normally be too risky. The grounds for this approach are that if you hit you will get a break out of it. If you miss, you have merely saved your opponent 1 bisque. There is some psychological advantage as well, especially if you hit in. Only do this when you know that if you hit in, you can make a break from it.

When your opponent only has a few bisques, either left or to start with, play as though you were even. Do exercise more care on your leaves, however.

What else?

You are now on your way down. Study this chapter and put these tactics into play. Play many games and practice on your weak points. It will then not be long before you get to single figures. The next step is to 8 and you will have left C class play behind, and be ready for chapter 4.

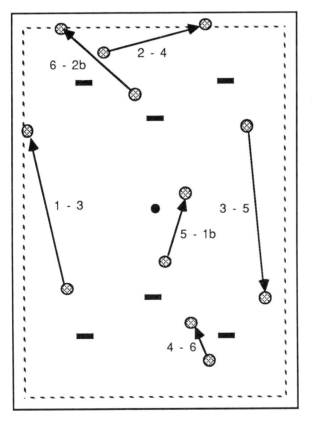

Note.

1 - 3 = The Ball at
hoop 1 being
sent as a
pioneer to
hoop 3.

Fig 3.1 (a)   Rush points for a three ball break (first 6 hoops).

63

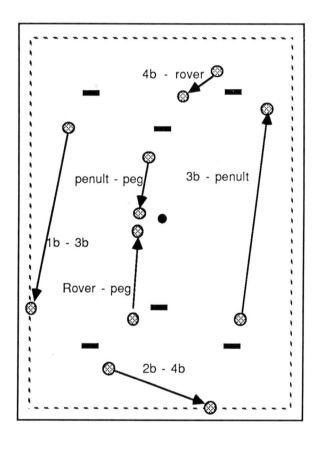

Fig 3.1 (b)   Rush points for a three ball break (second 6 hoops).

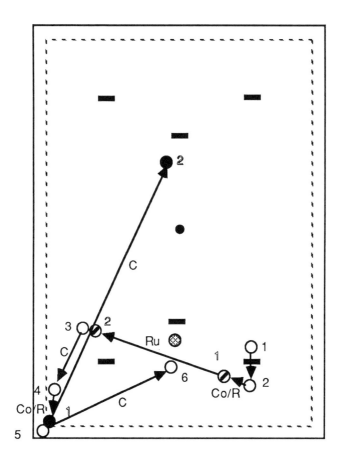

Fig 3.2.1 (i)   Picking up a ball in Corner 1 after hoop 4.

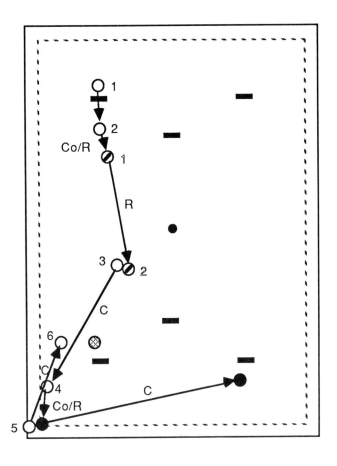

Fig 3.2.1 (ii)   Picking up a ball in Corner 1 after 1 back.

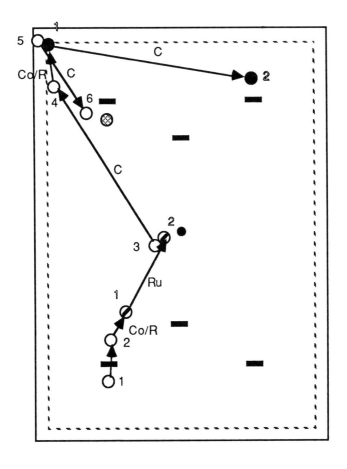

Fig 3.2.2 (i)   Picking up a ball in Corner 2 after hoop 1.

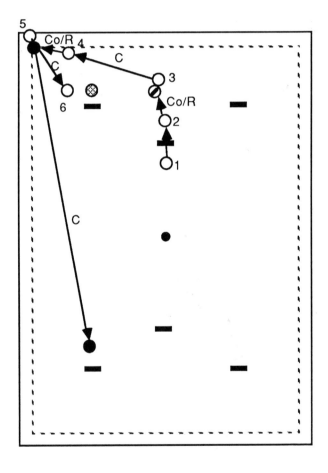

Fig 3.2.2 (ii)   Picking up a ball in Corner 2 after hoop 6.

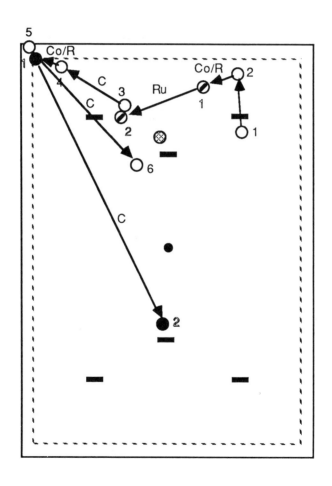

Fig 3.2.2 (iii)   Picking up a ball in Corner 2 after four back.

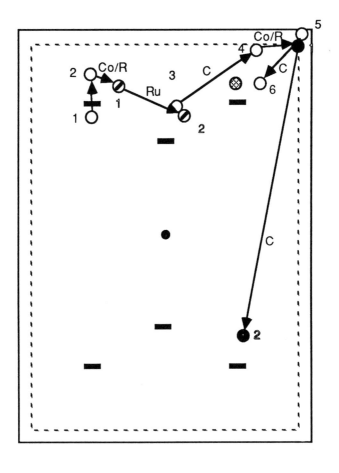

Fig 3.2.3 (i) Picking up a ball in Corner 3 after hoop 2.

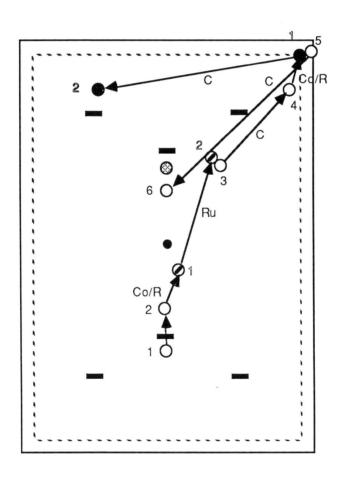

Fig 3.2.3 (ii)   Picking up a ball in Corner 3 after hoop 6.

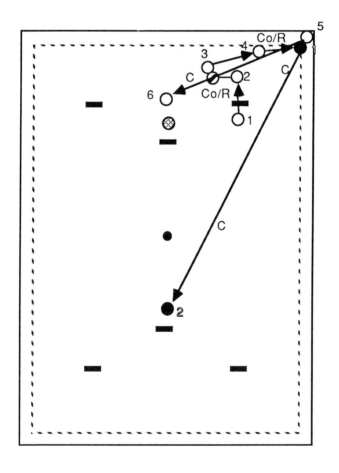

Fig 3.2.3 (iii)   Picking up a ball in Corner 3 after four back.

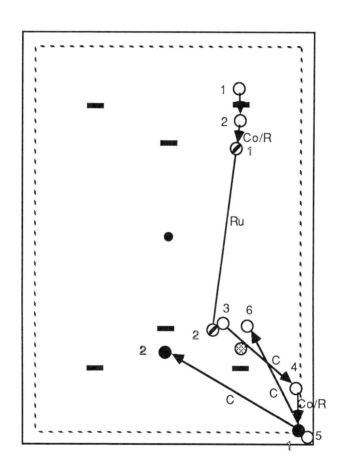

Fig 3.2.4 (i)   Picking up a ball in Corner 4 after hoop 3.

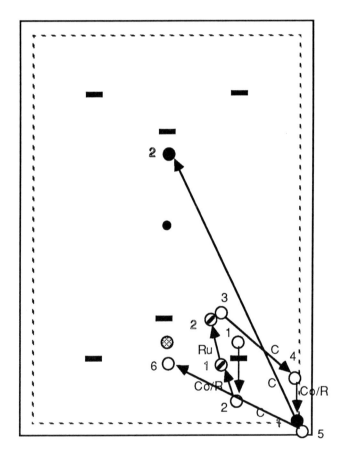

Fig 3.2.4 (ii)   Picking up a ball in Corner 4 after hoop 4.

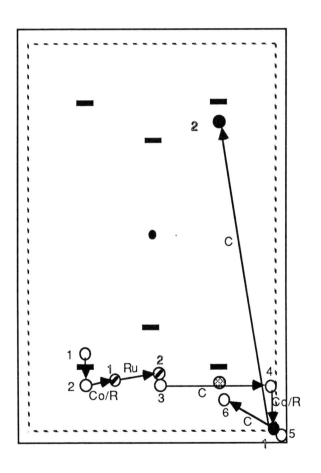

Fig 3.2.4 (iii)   Picking up a ball in Corner 4 after 2 back.

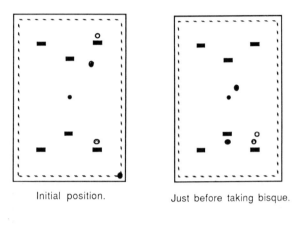

Initial position.   Just before taking bisque.

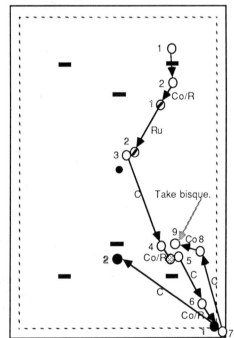

Fig 3.3   Picking up a ball in Corner 4, using a bisque.

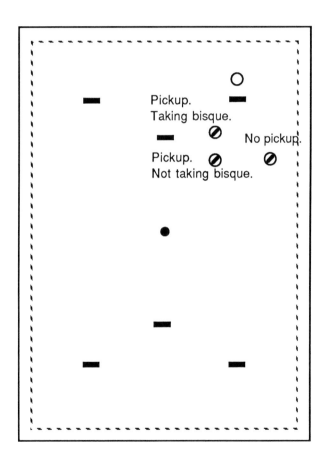

Fig 3.4   Positions for various options.

GET SET!

Chapter 4

Go!

*T*o use this chapter you will have a handicap between 8 and 6. You should therefore:

● Understand all but the more obscure rules and definitions of croquet.

● Know when to call a referee and be considering becoming a referee yourself.

● Have read the rules of croquet (but not necessarily the regulations) as published by the CA and understood most of them.

● Be able to play within the above rules and know what action to take if any of those rules are transgressed.

● Be able to play hampered and jump shots confidently.

● Understand, and put into practice, the information contained in chapters 2 and 3.

If you feel unsure about any of the above points, you should study or practice as appropriate before proceeding further.

Your picture of yourself

You are now progressing through the B class handicap range. You will be very likely to find a little hiccup in your progress towards the A class. The main reason for this is that you are now giving bisques as often as you receive them. As a consequence of this, you having to learn how to play on your own merits much more. You are also having to learn defensive play against other beginners who are as you used to be. So you may feel that you have stuck at around 7 or 8. Do not get too disheartened, you will soon come out of it.

You will have noticed that the previous two chapters each had a theme. In chapter 2 it was "understand your own and your opponents' abilities." Chapter 3 concentrated on "planning your game." The theme of this chapter is "assessing the risk." Many times on previous pages you have seen "assess the risk and play accordingly." This is all very well but how do you do it? You will base your decision on the following three questions.

Will I make this shot successfully?

If I do, what can I make from it?

If I do not, what will my opponent make from it?

Understanding your abilities will help you answer the first and second questions, while understanding your opponent will help answer the third. Planning your game will reduce the number of times you ask the questions!

What I will look at in this chapter is a means whereby you can link together the likely answers to these questions. You can then make a balanced decision. It is based on mathematical probability, but don't worry, there is nothing very theoretical! Please do note the comment which I repeat later on in this chapter. This is that the tables and calculations are designed to help you in a practice situation. You will then get a "feel" for risk. In a real game there is not time for complicated calculations.

Probability concerns itself with the likelihood of something happening (or not). It is expressed in several ways but the only one I shall use is the "one in x" way. This means that something will happen on average once every x times. Thus a one in two probability means that on average something will occur once every two operations. An example is when spinning a coin. Notice that I have said "on average." You well know that spinning a coin may result in several heads coming up in succession. If you spin a hundred times however, you will get close to 50 heads and 50 tails. I will ignore the probability of it landing on its side!

A probability of one in one is a certainty, i.e. it must happen. There are very few things that are certain, but many which are so close that are considered so.

A probability of one in infinity is an impossibility, i.e. it cannot happen. For example, the probability of finishing first turn is one in infinity.

The probability is that you are wondering just where this is all leading to! — Probably!!

To clear the air a bit, let's consider three situations. In each, it is your turn, and you have to decide what you are going to do. Let me say right away, there will be no "right answer." There seldom is, but there is usually an answer (or sometimes answers) which represents the smallest risk, balanced against the greatest gain. So we look at probability, which helps to assess the risk.

Situation 1, Figure 4.1.

Your opponent is for hoop 2 and rover. You are for 4 back and hoop 1. Your forward ball is by hoop 2 and the other in the middle. Your opponent lays up near corner 4 with a rush to hoop 3. You can see all balls but have no double. It is your turn. There are no bisques. You are an 8 and playing well, your opponent is a 16 and playing poorly.

Situation 2, Figure 4.2.

Your opponent is for hoop 2 and hoop 3 back. You are for 6 and rover. Your forward ball is in corner 1 and the other by hoop 3. Your opponent has clanged hoop 2, is cross wired at 2, and has two bisques left. It is your turn. You are an 8 and playing poorly, your opponent is a 14 and playing averagely.

Situation 3, Figure 4.3.

You are all for penultimate. Your balls are near penult and rover, separated by about 10 yards and half pegged from each other. Your opponent is on the north boundary in front of 1 back and on the south boundary in front of 3 back. There are no bisques and it is again your turn. You are an 8 and your opponent is a 2. You are both playing fairly well.

Here are three situations, all very different and all requiring a decision. Before I go into each one in detail, it is necessary to consider some typical probabilities.

GO!

a.   The single ball roquet.

You will know the distance over which you can virtually guarantee a roquet. To make life simpler I will call that distance D. We can assume then that at any distance less than D, the probability of hitting is one in one. This I will show as 1:1. What if we have a ball at twice D? The probability is now 1:2 (one in two) For those interested in proof, draw a line on a piece of paper showing your ball just missing the target at distance D. Then extend the line to 2D and measure the error distance (remember to include half the width of the striking ball). From this information I have derived the following table. This gives probabilities for different distances greater than D, with an example where D is 8 yards.

Distance to ball.	Example distance.	Probability of hitting.
D	8 yards	1:1
D x 1.25	10 yards	4:5
D x 1.5	12 yards	2:3
D x 1.75	14 yards	4:7
D x 2	16 yards	1:2
D x 3	24 yards	1:3
D x 4	32 yards	1:4

This table takes no account of such things as variations of slope and texture on the lawn. Or that on long shots you have to hit harder, perhaps spoiling your aim. These things will make the probability of hitting worse rather than better. It would be impossible to show just how much worse. In any case the figures are only a guide, so I have chosen to stay with the simple approach.

b.   Single peg target.

The peg is a smaller target than a ball. Obviously the distance over which you can guarantee a hit is less than D. The maths show that for practical purposes the distance is three quarters of D. So in the previous example where D is 8 yards, D(peg) is 6 yards. Exactly the same rules apply as in (a) e.g. at 18 yards (D(peg) x 3) the probability is 1:3. Thus a ball 10 yards from you is a better target than the peg at 9 yards. On the other hand, the peg at 9 yards is a better target than a ball at 14 yards.

So a simple rule of thumb is this. You have a choice between the peg and a ball. If the peg is less than three quarters of the distance to the ball, shoot at the peg. If it is greater, shoot at the ball.

c.   Partly wired ball.

For a partly hidden ball, where you can only hit one side of it, D reduces considerably. The table below gives values for D for different amounts of ball showing. In brackets are the amounts which that will mean when D is 8 yards.

> With half or more of the ball showing — D reduces to a quarter (2 yards).
> With a quarter of the ball showing — D reduces to an eighth (1 yard).
> With an eighth of the ball showing — D reduces to a sixteenth (1.5 feet).

d.   More than one ball with no gap greater than a ball width between them.

The limit to this situation occurs when you have three balls in line, each separated by just less than a ball width. This is an equivalent target of 5 balls. The formula for working out the new value of D is this.

New value of D = Original value of D times (half the target width in balls + a half).

Examples (D = 8 yards in brackets) ,

● You can see a ball and a half.
$$D(new) = D \times (0.75 + 0.5)$$
$$= D \times 1.25 \qquad (10 \text{ yards})$$
● You can see two balls together.
$$D(new) = D \times (1 + 0.5)$$
$$= D \times 1.5 \qquad (12 \text{ yards})$$
● You can see 2 balls a ball apart.
$$D(new) = D \times (1.5 + 0.5)$$
$$= D \times 2 \qquad (16 \text{ yards})$$

e.   Two/three balls more than a ball apart.

This is a complicated situation, so let's consider the easy options first.

If the distance to the nearest ball is D yards or less, then go for a single ball.

If the distance between the balls is greater than a yard, go for a single ball.

If neither of the above applies, use the following approximate formula.

If the gap between the balls in ball widths is greater than the number of times D that you are from the target, shoot for a single ball, otherwise shoot for the middle of the gap.

Note that if you are able to shoot for the gap, it roughly doubles the probability of hitting.

Example 1. Two balls a foot apart, you are 16 yards away, D = 8 yards.

The gap is about three balls, you are twice D away, so shoot for the single target.

Example 2.

Two balls 15 inches apart, you are 32 yards away, D = 8 yards.

The gap is about four balls, you are four times D away so shoot for the gap. The probability of hitting is about 1:2.

f.   Rushing and cut rushing.

There is no point in attempting to be scientific about rushing distance. It varies so much and has so many factors. All that you can do is to practice accuracy and strength on your own lawn. Then modify this according to the conditions.

Cut rushing is difficult — but is a boon when you can do it accurately. I would recommend that you do not try for cut rushes with accuracy over a distance greater than a sixteenth of D. Do not try approximate cuts (in the general direction that you want) over a distance greater than an eighth of D.

g. Getting position for a rush from a take-off, or croquet stroke.

Warning. Although (a) to (e) are guidelines only, they do have a fair basis of fact. This section merely gives a rough idea of what to expect.

Choose a convenient distance, D is as good as any. See how accurate you are in terms of angle and distance judging at that distance. Then for any multiple of D your accuracy will be that much worse (approximately).

Example, D = 8 yards. At that distance in a croquet stroke you are accurate to 2 feet on distance and 1 foot on angle. At 24 yards you will be approximately accurate to 6 feet on distance and 3 feet on angle.

Now, considering the examp.......

"Wait just a cotton-pickin minute Mr Gaunt!"

"Yes, dear Reader?"

"You do not seriously expect me to take this book on to the lawn do you? There I will sit for half an hour each turn, working out all these figures. Then I will decide on the best shot?"

"No, of course I don't. To start with it would be illegal because that is using an artificial aid. The purpose is to give you the information that you need. Eventually you will be able to size up a situation with confidence, rather than trusting to luck."

"So the tables above are of no real value?"

"Yes they are. Not being able to use them in a match does not mean that you cannot use them for practice. Even better would be for two of you to play a game where each turn you assess and discuss. If there is disagreement as to the best shot, try both and see if you can decide which offered the best chances. By doing this you will get a 'feel' for risks. After a while you will make many decisions without having to think mechanically about them. Can I get back to the book now?"

GO!

"Yes of course, be my guest!"

OK, so let's look at those examples again.

Situation 1.

Your opponent is for hoop 2 and rover. You are for 4 back and hoop 1. Your forward ball is by hoop 2 and the other in the middle. Your opponent lays up near corner 4 with a rush to hoop 3. You can see all balls but have no double. It is your turn. There are no bisques. You are an 8 and playing well, your opponent is a 16 and playing poorly.

The most likely situation here is that your opponent has used all of the bisques in several turns, has got one ball round and has managed a reasonable leave. You have had the innings a few times and have put together a few nice breaks. You want to move your forward ball for safety and the backward one for breaks. Assume that D for you is 5 yards while you estimate D for your opponent at 3 yards.

Let us eliminate the poor options. Joining up is suicide either way. Shooting at your opponent with the backward ball gives only about a 1:4 chance of hitting (there is no double remember). It leaves an easy break for your opponent if you miss. Shooting at your opponent with the forward ball gives about a 1:6 chance of hitting. You have a fair chance of a hoop or two for a hit, and a fairly difficult break (for a 16) for a miss.

You could play safe with the backward ball, and put it in corner 1. Your opponent will have 1 easy hoop and a good chance of a lay up afterwards. Playing safe with the forward ball leaves little for the opponent.

Shooting at your forward ball with the backward gives about a 1:2 chance of hitting. You have a good chance of a break if you hit, and a probable couple of hoops away if you miss.

Shooting at your backward ball with the forward gives about a 1:2 chance of hitting. You have a moderate chance of a break for a hit, and little away for a miss.

So, what should you do? I would go for the backward ball with the forward. The chances of hitting are fair, of reward good, and of penalties small. If I wasn't hitting too well then I would play safe with the forward ball.

Situation 2.

Your opponent is for hoop 2 and hoop 3 back. You are for 6 and rover. Your forward ball is in corner 1 and the other by hoop 3. Your opponent has clanged hoop 2, is cross wired at 2, and has two bisques left. It is your turn. You are an 8 and playing poorly, your opponent is a 14 and playing averagely.

Here it would appear that you started well with every intention of steamrollering your opponent by + 26. Indeed you got the first ball round. Then it all went wrong and now you have lost your accuracy and your confidence. Your opponent meanwhile has kept at it steadily and has not used the bisques. This has kept pressure on you and prevented you from rash attempts at a break. Your opponent now still refuses to take a bisque because the set up is not good, being wired.

There is little choice but to move your backward ball because leaving it at 3 is suicidal. The chance of hitting either of the opponent's balls is small. Anyway, she/he is wired. The choice here is to join up in corner 1. This move will almost certainly force the use of a bisque. So you might as well shoot for your ball rather than have a wide join.

Situation 3.

You are all for penultimate. Your balls are near penult and rover, separated by about 10 yards and half pegged from each other. Your opponent is on the north boundary in front of 1 back and on the south boundary in front of 3 back. There are no bisques and it is again your turn. You are an 8 and your opponent is a 2. You are both playing fairly well.

There are no other wired balls apart from your own partial peg hamper. If we assume that D for you is about 5 yards, the chance of hitting your own ball is about 1:7, which is poor. Also, a miss will give the opponent an easy pickup. The chance of hitting either of your opponent's balls (from the closest ball in each case) is about 1:3. However, shooting with the ball at penult gives a poorer chance of a break to your opponent if you miss.

It also gives a poorer chance to you if you hit. Remember that the opponent is a 2 and is playing fairly well, so the risk is high. The best option is to play safe, and the ball at penult the one to move, but where to? The best shot for the opponent (if the ball at penult is simply removed) to play would be at the ball near the peg. A miss will go through to her/his own ball on the north boundary. A good defensive position would therefore be to put the ball which is at penult in corner 3. This may well force your opponent to play safe as well, giving you breathing space.

Your picture of your opponent.

Add to the things that you already look for, an assessment of your opponent's risk-judging capability. You may well be able to capitalise on your opponent being over- or under-cautious. Beware of making a false assessment. If your opponent keeps going for "suicide" shots and getting them it is no use leaving a deliberate "suicide" tempter.

The two ball break.

The main reason for your doing a two ball break will be because of the awkward placing of the other balls when you have no bisques left.

A two ball break is simple in concept but difficult in execution. You have a ball at your hoop, but no pivot or pioneer. So when you run a hoop, the following rush has got to get your ball to the next hoop. The trick is to make that rush as simple as possible. To achieve THAT needs accurate placing of the ball past the hoop that you are about to run. It also needs accurate hoop running. Unlike the four and three ball breaks, you should aim to get the ball some way past the hoop. A suitable position is 5 yards, and on the appropriate side. This makes the chances of getting a good rush easier. Note that when going straight down the lawn, e.g. hoop 1 to hoop 2, your forward ball should not be to one side. Two ball breaks are not easy, but are worth practicing because they are often used to start a three or four ball. The easiest two ball run is from hoop 4 to 1 back.

The four ball break.

You will be making four ball breaks with confidence now. You will often go all the way round as far as you want. Here are a couple of tips which make the four ball just a little easier to execute. Figures 4.4 and 4.5 illustrate them.

i   After running hoop 4, you will approach the pivot ball. Do so in a way that will enable you to leave it about halfway between hoop 5 and peg. Approach hoop 5 as normal, but run the hoop a little harder to reach the pivot. Roquet the pivot and croquet it to 2 back, giving yourself a rush with the ball near hoop 5 towards the peg. Croquet this ball to 1 back, approaching the pioneer at hoop 6.

Approach hoop 6 sending the croqueted ball to the left. When you run hoop 6 you can rush to the boundary in front of 1 back. Take croquet and send the ball to half way between 1 back and 2 back, approaching 1 back.

ii.   Approach 1 back sending the croqueted ball to the right. Then you can rush to near the ball which is halfway to 2 back. Take croquet and send the ball to peg to restore the pivot. Also get a rush (with the ball which is halfway to 2 back) to the boundary near to 2 back. Send the ball to 3 back and approach 2 back. Continue the four ball break.

Playing with and without bisques.

a.   Many bisques (6 or more).

Notice that "many bisques" is now defined as 6 or more. This is because you will now be so good at using them that a single bisque is very powerful. If you have 6 or more bisques then you will be playing someone who is good, probably a minus player. So you are looking towards getting both balls to peg and still having bisques left.

You will notice that this chapter says much less than the previous two about the use of bisques. This is because most of what there is to say on the subject was covered in the previous chapters. Also, you are now giving bisques as often as you receive them. Your play is becoming much more dependent on your own ability rather than on handicap.

b. Giving bisques.

In the last chapter I gave some advice on tactics. This explained how to counter some of the methods used against you to extract bisques or force you into an error. I repeat them here, but this time it is you who are doing the extracting! Of course your opponent may have read this book as well and be aware of the tactics. That does not mean that they will not still be effective.

1. Go, or get put in, first and lay a very short tice.

If your opponent hits, and,

a. Rolls both balls to the middle, then put your ball to corner 4.

b. Puts one ball near hoop 2 and the other in the middle then shoot through to corner 2.

c. Puts one ball in corner 1 and one in corner 3. If you can get a rush on one of the balls, rush it up the court. Then take off to the other one, sending that down the boundary. Finally put your ball to corner 4. If all this looks too difficult, go to corner 4 anyway.

2. Shoot deliberately to miss at the first ball in or near corner 4. Leave a double when you replace your ball. This is quite a good opening gambit, but you should not try it if you are a poor hitter.

What happens next depends on the way the balls end up after your opponent has played the third ball. Whatever happens you should get some shot that is worth taking.

3. During the game leave "tempters." These are ball positions from which it would be possible (but not easy) to set up a four ball break. Or they are likely (but not certain) to give you a good break next time. That is, if your opponent does not hit in or take a bisque.

What else?

By now you will have realised that I have only just scratched the surface of croquet tactics. You will have worked out some of your own, disagreed with some of mine, and been told others by your friends. Soon you will be ready to tackle the A class. If you are succesful, you will learn yet more tactics, particularly those of advanced play. Study the auxiliary chapters which follow, if you haven't already, and good luck in the A Class!

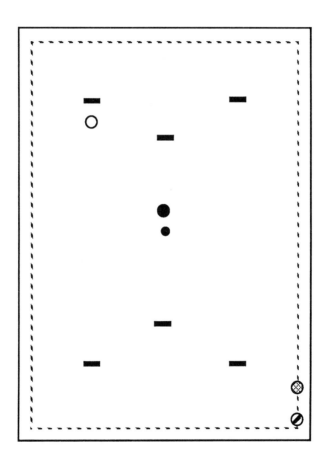

Fig 4.1   Situation 1.

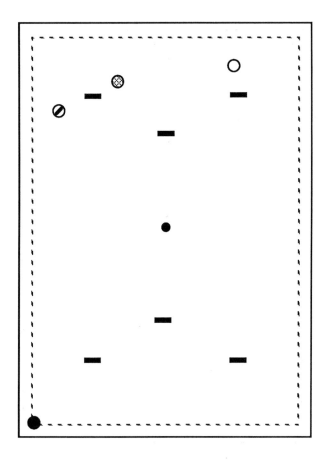

Fig 4.2   Situation 2.

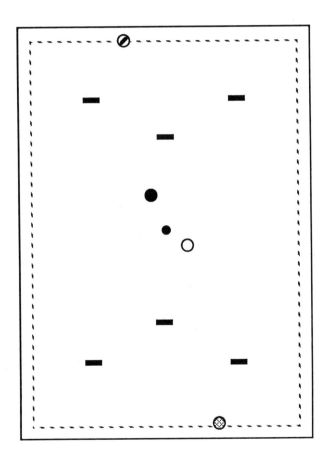

Fig 4.3   Situation 3.

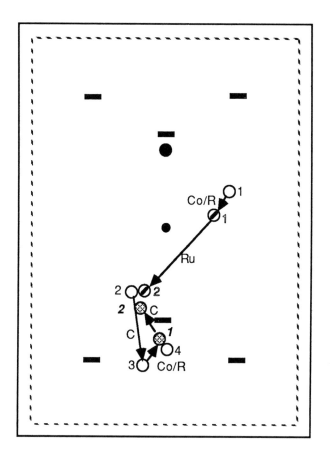

Fig 4.4   Simplification of the four ball break (i).

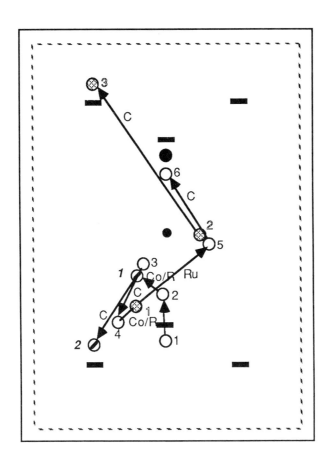

Fig 4.4 (a)   Simplification of the four ball break (i continued).

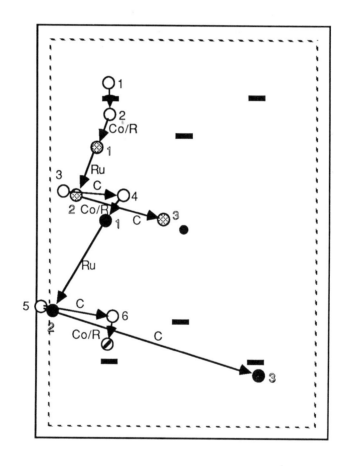

Fig 4.5   Simplification of the four ball break (ii).

Chapter 5

The End Game

*T*owards the end of the first season and after a coaching session, Jill and Celia were talking about the game.

"You know what," they said, "We have learnt a lot about shots, etc., and how to play breaks. However, we don't know how to finish properly. The result of this is that we often only win games by one point after Time."

Thus the name of the book, and the title of this chapter.

Untimed games and timed games with a lot of time left.

A few points about the law on pegging out.

Only a rover ball can peg out another rover ball. This rule is absolute for all versions of the game. If the ball you are playing with has not completed all of its hoops, it cannot peg out any ball. It cannot of course, peg out itself.

In handicap games (the only ones considered in this book) both of your balls MUST be rovers before you can peg one or both out. BUT.... But if you peg out an opponent's ball which is a rover, you CAN peg your own out as well. This is irrespective of the position of your other ball.

The normal finish sequence is one where you have a rush with one of your balls on the other, towards the peg. Take the rush, sending the ball to near the peg. In the croquet stroke, send the forward ball on to the peg. In the continuation shot send.your playing ball on to the peg, having first removed the already pegged out ball.

● What happens if in the rush to the peg, your rushed ball hits the peg? This is sometimes called a "Grievous," because if this happens your turn ends. Why? Because the rush has pegged out your forward ball, so you have nothing from which to take croquet!

● What happens if during the croquet stroke your forward ball hits the peg, then bounces back and hits your struck ball? Nothing, carry on with the continuation shot from wherever the struck ball ends up. Why? Because the pegged out ball is still "live" until it has stopped moving.

● What happens if during the croquet stroke, both balls hit the peg? Both balls are then pegged out.

Positioning your ball for a peg out.

In the following situations I will call one ball, which is the one that you are striking, the Striker's Ball (SB). The other (which is your partner ball) I will call the Peg Ball (PB).

a.   From a four ball break, Figures 5.1.i to 5.1.iiib.

Assume that you are in a break, and are in front of 4 back. PB will be in one of the three positions of the break. These are near peg, near penult, or behind 4 back.

i.   Near peg. This is the easiest position to have. All that you need to do is maintain the break, giving yourself a short rush back to PB after running rover.

ii.   Near penult. In the croquet stroke when approaching penult, send PB about 8 ft beyond penult. It should be on the same side as the pivot ball. Run the hoop and rush to the pivot. Croquet PB to near (about 1 — 2 yards) peg, roquet the pivot and continue.

iii.   (a).   Behind 4 back. Rush PB to near peg. Take off to the old pivot and rush it to rover and take off to penult. Or rush to just past penult and drive it to rover, approaching penult.

iii (b).   Here is an alternative worth considering if you spot that this situation will occur. When you approach three back, place the croqueted ball to the left. Having run three back, croquet to rover, going to the pivot with SB. Then rush the pivot to penult and take off to four back. Although this shot involves a split shot and a rush, they are only short ones. It then means that you can put PB straight to peg when you have run four back.

So, as you can see, there is not much to worry about in a straightforward four ball situation. The third situation is perhaps a little tricky, but just needs care.

b. From a three ball break.

Again assume that you are in front of 4 back. PB will be behind 4 back, near penult, or somewhere else (probably on a boundary or in a corner).

i. Behind 4 back, Figure 5.2. Pick up the spare ball either directly or with a bisque if you can. If not, you will have to continue with the three ball break. This will mean that you will put PB near rover after you have run four back. After running penult, rush to near rover. Croquet the ball just past rover and approach PB with your ball. Roquet PB then croquet it just to one side of rover putting SB in front of it. Run rover, roquet the ball past the hoop and take off to give yourself a rush to peg using PB.

ii. Near penult. Continue with the three ball, putting PB near peg after penult.

iii. Somewhere else (for diagrams, see the examples). Its placing is awkward or you would have picked it up before. The assumption must also be that you have only 1 bisque or none left. Otherwise you would set up a four ball break.

If you have one bisque left, continue with the three ball unless making a four ball is simple. When you run penult, rush to near rover and croquet that ball a short distance (3 -5 yards) towards PB. Approach and run rover off the pioneer. In the hoop approach, put the croqueted ball on the same side of rover as the ball which you sent towards PB. Run the hoop and make the roquet. Play the next croquet stroke to get a rush towards PB with the ball that you sent in that direction. Get a rush on PB towards peg if you can otherwise roll up towards peg, take position and the bisque, and finish.

If you have no bisques, you should play in much the same way as the previous paragraph. In addition try for two things.

(a) to get the rush on PB to peg and

(b) leave your opponent widely separated.

If you achieve (a) & (b) take the rush and try to peg out both. Do a soft croquet stroke. Then if you fail to peg out the PB, it will still be close to the peg. You should peg out SB anyway.

If you achieve (a) but not (b) take the rush but try for a firm peg out with PB. This will put the croqueted ball near the boundary (but not off or near any other ball). Do not peg out SB if you fail, but put it away into a corner somewhere.

If you achieve (b) but not (a) roll up to the peg and peg SB out. Or if you cannot do good rolls, lay yourself a rush to peg from a safe spot. Make sure that you do not leave a double.

If you get one ball pegged out and your opponent hits in or you hit in against someone who has done this to you, see the chapter on pegged out games.

To achieve (a) & (b), set up the balls as they were described in the situation when you had one bisque. This time when you have run rover you should be able to rush the ball which is beyond rover. Rush it to a point where you can croquet it to a safe position. You will still need to get the rush towards PB. Here are two examples. One has the PB in corner 4 and one has the ball on the West boundary opposite hoop 2. I have called the opponent's balls OB1 & OB2.

A, Figure 5.3. (PB in Corner 4, OB1 between penult and Peg, OB2 in front of rover and SB in front of penult). Run penult and rush OB1 to between peg and rover. Croquet OB1 to just short of hoop 4 getting position with SB on OB2. Roquet OB2, croquet OB2 to 6 ft past rover and approach rover with SB. Run rover and rush OB2 to halfway between OB1 and PB. Drive OB2 to just past hoop 2 getting a rush with SB on OB1 to PB. Rush to the boundary near PB. Replace the balls on the yard line and take off to get the rush on PB.

B, Figure 5.4. (PB on W Boundary nr hoop 2, OB1, OB2 & SB as before). Run penult and rush OB1 6 ft past rover. Drive OB1 to halfway between hoops 2 & 6 getting position on OB2. Roquet OB2 and croquet it to about 4 ft past rover on the RHS. Approach rover with SB and run it. Rush OB2 to near hoop 2. Drive OB2 to just past hoop 4 getting a rush with SB on OB1 to PB. Rush to boundary near PB, replace balls on yard line and take off to get the rush on PB.

If during any of this you get a cannon shot, treat as described in the chapter on helpful hints.

c.   From a two ball break.

This is not as rare as you might think. In the end game both players are being ultra careful, especially if the scores are similar. So there is often very little chance of making a break. I will assume that the bisques have gone. If they haven't, then don't think of two ball breaks! With care, you can start a two ball from four back, but any more than that is difficult.

There are two situations, described as follows, but only proceed with the break if you are confident of not breaking down. If breaking down seems likely, lay up somewhere safe.

i.   One ball is not yours. The finish after rover is much the same as for a finish in a three ball situation. Take due note of the position of the other two balls.

ii.   Both balls are yours. Approach rover with the croquet stroke. Then send PB to a position level with rover and about a foot to one side. Run rover gently and you should have a good rush to peg.

d.   From a hit in when both your balls are for peg.

i.   You hit an opponent's ball. Set up a finish as described for the three ball situation. You may or may not be able to finish depending on how the balls land up.

ii.   You hit the PB. You probably will not be able to finish from here, so split the opponent and lay a rush. If you can get it, a rush from halfway down the W or E boundaries is a good place. Watch out for leaving the double!

THE END GAME

Timed Games.

A few points about keeping time. Make sure that you and your opponent know and agree what the time limit is. One of you be the time keeper. Make a note of your start time and check that your opponent agrees. Keep a track of any delays. Only include delays that are agreed by the tournament manager or deputy. Do not make your own up, even if you feel that you are treated unfairly.

At about 10 minutes before Time is due, ask someone to call time. Say clearly when time is up and ask them to call TIME in a clear voice, EXACTLY on time. To simplify the words that follow, I am referring to the action of calling time as just Time.

Do not start to worry about the end of the game too soon. Remember that it only takes about 20 minutes to do an all round break. On the other hand it is easy to spend 20 minutes "wallying around" getting nowhere. As a general rule, start looking at the situation when there is about half an hour to go.

a. You are in front.

If you are a long way in front with 30 minutes to go, you should start to play defensively. Play in such a way that you prevent your opponent from picking up an easy break. This does not mean playing "Aunt Emma," it means not taking risks that you might have done earlier in the game. You do not want to leave an easy pick up for your opponent. The amount of care that you exercise increases as you get closer to Time. At around 10 minutes to go the care exercised is such that you do virtually play Aunt Emma tactics. This is not nice but is essential here.

If you are not a long way in front with 30 minutes to go, it is too soon to start considering end tactics. You should play your normal game. At 15 minutes to go, start playing as in the previous paragraph, i.e. with increasing care.

You are now at what you consider to be your last turn. If you are a long way ahead, then extend that to your last two or three turns. Separate your opponent if you can, and place your balls in unwanted corners. Apart from any "free" shots that you might get presented with, do not come out of these corners.

b.   You are behind.

If you are a long way behind with 30 minutes to go, you should start to take risks. At this stage the risks need not be too great, but as Time gets closer, you will need to take more. Now, "taking risks" does not mean going mad! It means that you go for roquets slightly longer than you would normally try. Or you attempt hoops with more angle than you prefer, etc. When there are only 10 minutes or less left and you are still a long way behind — anything goes! You have no choice but to try the impossible. When trying it, try properly because it might work. For example, suppose that the best shot that you have available to you is a 10 yard hoop. Do not randomly "hack" at it, but line up carefully and play with moderate strength. It might go — you might make the next roquet — YOU MIGHT WIN!! However you probably won't!

If you are not a long way behind, then forget the time. Do not rush around like a scalded cat, making wild shots and moaning about the slowness of your opponent. This will only serve to guarantee your losing. If your opponent really IS wasting time, call a referee.

Tied games.

Here is the law. A tied (but not finished) game is one where at the end of the last turn at Time, the number of points scored by each side is the same. There is a very strict definition about which is the last turn. You should know about it because it is not the same as the normal definition for end of turn. Nor, as we shall see, is the last turn necessarily the final turn of the game. To explain it here are some examples.

i.   Time occurs just as or after you hit a ball. That ball then makes a valid roquet or hoop. — Your turn continues. It is your last turn and you cannot take any more bisques during it. Your opponent has one more turn but cannot take bisques. If the scores are even, it is a tied game.

ii.   As (i) above but you fail to make the roquet or hoop. Your turn ends. Your opponent has one more turn then so do you. Neither of you can take bisques. If the scores are even, the game is tied.

103

iii.   Time occurs just before you hit the ball. This is your last turn whether you score a point or not. Your opponent has one more turn.

iv.   You claim a bisque just before Time. You may take the bisque but no more. It is your last turn, your opponent then has one more turn.

v.   In all other situations where you are in the middle of your turn, you complete that turn. Your opponent then has one more turn. As before, neither of you can take bisques after Time.

Apart from the rather complicated ruling, we always end up with one of two situations. You either get another go or you don't! From this it follows that either you or your opponent will get the last turn depending on the situation. It might seem that you always want to end up getting the last turn, but that is not necessarily so. Let us consider the situations.

If you are behind, you may see that this will be your last turn if you try a break to catch up. You have two choices.

i.   You go all out for as many hoops as you can this turn, playing carefully and ignoring Time. If you are playing with the backward ball and still cannot make enough points to get a tie or to go ahead, you will have to do some peels as well.

ii.   You play quickly to split your opponent constructively, and lay up a break for your last turn. Only use this second option when you really have nothing suitable with which to make a break. Or you are playing with the forward ball and cannot make enough hoops to get a tie or go ahead.

Remember the following points about the "last" turn when it is yours.

a.   If you get the lead, having been behind, you are certain of winning.

b.   If you stay behind you have certainly lost.

c.   If you get a tie, the last turn is no longer the final turn, see "Resolving a tie." It might be the best thing to do, get a tie, if the next point is very difficult. Then lay up a rush for the point when resolving the tie.

d.   Remember, when both balls are not for peg, you cannot peg your playing ball out to get that extra point that you need to tie or win.

e.   Even if you are in front, when entitled to a last turn, you may take it. In fact if you peg out in this turn you have a win and not a win on time. Also it may be worth getting a few more points in case you need them to resolve the tournament winner.

If you are in front, only go for safe, easy hoops. Leave your opponent a very difficult task to pick up a break, as previously described.

A word about "time wasting." There is nothing in the rules that says that the person in the lead has to play any faster than normal. It is no use muttering under your breath at perfectly reasonable lengths of time to take shots. However there IS a rule about taking more time than is reasonable. You can call a referee if you think that this is happening. Be careful though, since some players are slower than others. It would not be proper to call attention to slow play at the end of a game when you have tolerated the same speed of play up to now without complaint. Also, remember that when you are itching to get on, everything else seems to conspire to slow you. This may well extend to a double-banked game, where the other game seems intent on holding you up! Although some referees may allow extra time for delay due to the other game, others may not. It is their decision and you must accept it. Finally, remember that at Time, there is no further pressure. So if you are hurrying to finish a break before time, but cannot, stop for a few seconds at Time. Look at the situation and evaluate what you do next. This is your last turn!

Resolving the tie.

So, here we are at Time. The last turn has finished and the scores are even. What happens now?

What happens is that play continues until one player scores a point. That player is then the winner by "PLUS ONE ON TIME!"

Remember that you only have to score just that one vital point, so forget about building breaks. Just look for the easiest way to score the point. If you can make a roquet but do not have a rush, consider a take-off. From there, take position in front of the hoop.

You are in front of your hoop, but at a very poor angle. You have separated your opponent. Consider going gently and sticking in the hoop.

If you are the separated one, you must judge if your opponent is likely to get the point next turn. If you think that the answer is yes, then shoot at the nearest ball, otherwise join wide.

In conclusion then, no-one likes a time limited game. They have to exist in order that managers can plan tournaments sensibly. Play at the end of a timed game is often far removed from that during normal circumstances. However, since a fair number of your games will finish this way, it is important to know what to do. A plus one on time win is still a win!

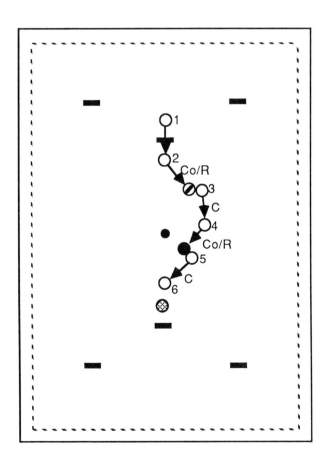

Fig 5.1.i   Positioning for the peg out, from penult to Rover, PB near peg.

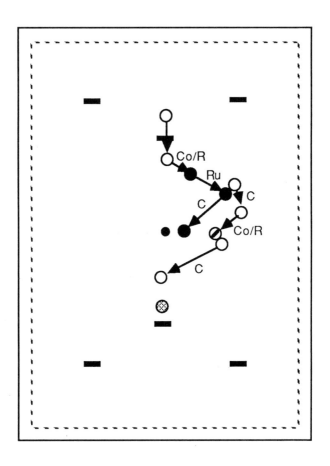

Fig 5.1.ii Positioning for the peg out, from penult to Rover, PB near penult.

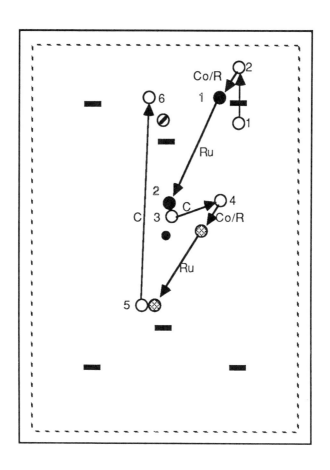

Figure 5.1.iiia.   Positioning for the peg out, from four back to penult, PB near four.

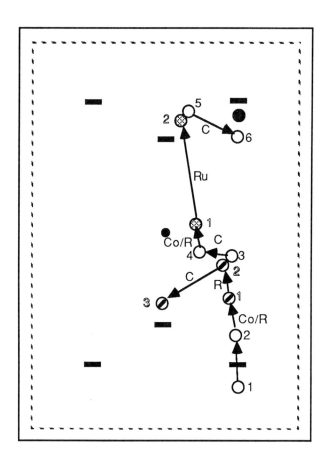

Fig 5.1.iiib.   Positioning for the peg out, from three back to four back, PB near four.

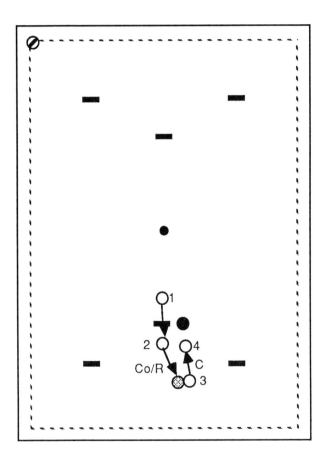

Fig 5.2   Positioning for the peg out, from Rover to peg, PB near four back.

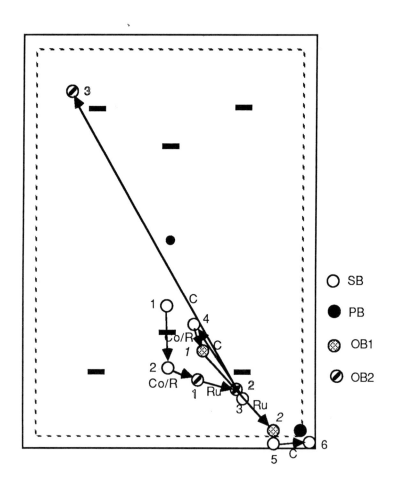

Fig 5.3   Positioning for the peg out, from Rover to peg, PB in corner four.

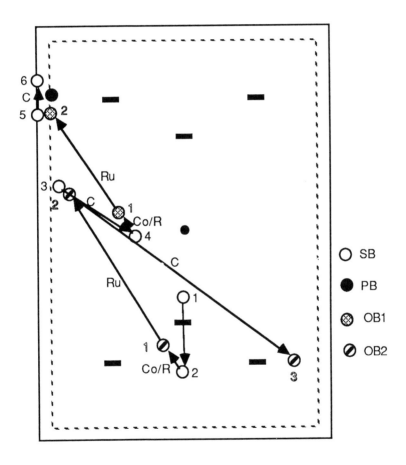

Fig 5.4   Positioning for the peg out, from Rover to peg, PB near hoop 2.

Chapter 6

Pegged Out and One-Ball Games

*A*pegged out game occurs when one of your or your opponent's balls becomes pegged out but not the other. A one-ball game occurs when you AND your opponent have just one ball left. Confusingly, some people refer to this as a two ball game (because there are two, not four, balls left). These types of game are usually short and often exciting, especially when both players know the tactics.

Pegged out games.

A. You are the one pegged out.

Do not panic and say "Oh I'll never win now." This is simply not true. I have won many games from this situation and lost many where I have pegged my opponent out. Let us however be realistic, the odds are often against you. Winning from this position, particularly if you have a lot of hoops to make, requires skill. It also needs tactics and a certain amount of luck. The skill you must acquire, the luck is outside your control and I discuss the tactics here.

There are three basic tactics when pegged out.

● Shoot — for a hoop or a ball.

● Lurk — near where you hope your opponent will break down.

● Position — in front of the hoop that you want.

Shoot.

This is what you will do wherever possible. You will also shoot under circumstances that you would never do normally. An example might be to shoot at a joined up opponent at or near the boundary. You need to ask yourself the question "Lurking or taking position are not suitable tactics. So can my opponent make an easy three ball break if I miss?" If the answer is no, shoot.

If you hit in, you must look to make the most of your chance, because you are unlikely to get many others. Can you get a three ball break from it? If not, can you make one hoop, then get a three ball? If not, can you get a two ball break? You will want the answer to be yes to one of these questions. If it is not then the tactic is as follows.

Having roqueted one ball, take off to the other. Give yourself a rush which will put the other ball to some point away from the hoop that you want. Make sure that it also separates your opponent. Take off for your hoop and run it if you can, or take position if you cannot. Do not do an enormous roll to your hoop as you will almost certainly fail. Then you will be unable to take position without giving your opponent an easy shot — a wasted hit in!

Figure 6.1 shows an example of the situation where you cannot sensibly make a break. You are for 1 back and in corner 3. Your opponent joined up near corner 4 and is for three back and peg. You shoot and hit but rush the ball some 5 yards away from its partner. You take off and try to get the rush to 1 back. However, you land short leaving a reasonable cut rush some 10 yards towards hoop 3 but nothing to 1 back. Take the rush and take off for one back. Take the hoop or position as appropriate. You are now in a fairly threatening position — think about it!

Chapter 2 contained the comment "If your opponent will certainly finish next turn, shoot, otherwise join up." This modifies to "otherwise decide whether to shoot, lurk or take position."

Lurk.

The best places to lurk are either in corners or on the boundaries parallel to hoops. Choose a point where you think that a breakdown by your opponent is most likely. This may not be the next hoop in order. For example, if your opponent has an easy rush to hoop 4, hoops 5, 6 and 1 back are all fairly easy. A lurk parallel to hoop 1 on the west boundary attacks 2 back and also gives good coverage of the middle hoops.

When should you lurk? When shooting is impossible or suicidal and taking position is pointless or suicidal. Remember that you do not actually have to hit a ball to take a shot. You may "deem" your ball struck, and hence leave it where it is.

Position.

I have already described one situation where you take position, under shooting. The other main time that you should do so is when you have your opponent separated, but you have no good shot. Of course you cannot do this if taking position gives your opponent an easy roquet. Then you have to shoot or lurk. Very occasionally you can do it to try to spoil your opponent's two ball by forcing him/her to come to move you. Perhaps you are for hoop 2 back and your opponent has a rush to hoop 2 from near hoop 3. These occasions are rare.

B.   You have pegged out your opponent.

Bearing in mind what was said in Chapter 2, and in section (A) above, be very careful about pegging out. Only do so when you are sure there is a positive advantage in doing so. It is very hard to give sound advice on this. It has been the subject of argument in Croquet Gazettes for years, and will probably continue for years to come. I pegged out an opponent once when he was at rover with the other ball. This was a very poor tactic. However for some reason it felt right to do so and indeed I won. That does not prove that I was right.

Having decided to peg out, how do you go about it? Remember the following points.

i   Never leave a double. Your opponent has little to lose now and will almost always shoot.

ii   If you have not roqueted your opponent's ball in that turn, you can wire yourself from it without conceding a lift.

iii   If you HAVE roqueted it, watch out that you do not give a lift!

iv   Avoid giving your opponent "free" shots. For example, avoid joining up in the middle.

117

v If you get into a tricky situation by accident, say you mess up the approach to penultimate and your opponent is for 6, use your continuation shot to get well away, and into a defensive position. Here for example, if your opponent's ball is near hoop 1, put your ball a little in from corner 3. Figure 6.2 illustrates the move. You can always join up next turn (but don't leave a double!).

One-ball Games.

Occasionally by design, and very occasionally by accident, the situation will arise where each side has one ball pegged out. If it happens by accident you will just have to play defensive or aggressive tactics (described below). These will vary according to the situation in which you find yourself.

You will do it by design when you have a significant lead with your remaining ball over the opponent's remaining ball. Here is a guide to significant leads.

Amount by which your handicap is greater (+) or less (−) than your opponent.	Number of points lead (or more) needed to consider pegging both balls out.
+ 15 to + 20	6
− 5 to + 14	5
− 12 to − 4	4

If your opponent has bisques left, add 2 points per bisque to the score possesed by your opponent. If you have bisques left, add 1 point per bisque to your score.

If the number of points left to score is less than the lead required, use the lower figure. Do not use less than 2 (except with bisques).

Do not count any point that you or your opponent will certainly make next turn. Say you are for 4 back and your opponent is dead in front of 2 back. Your lead is one not two.

Examples.

Suppose Bob, H/C 4 plays Faith, H/C 17. The difference is 13, so for Faith the normal lead she will require is 5, while for Bob it is 4.

A. Faith has no bisques left, she is for hoop 3, Bob is for 2 back.

Bob's lead is 5, he should peg both out.

B. As before but Faith has a bisque left.

Bob's effective lead is 3, he should not peg both balls out.

C. Faith has two bisques left, she is for hoop 5, Bob is for penult.

Bob has only two points to score, but adding 4 for the bisques makes an effective difference of only 1. He should not peg both balls out.

The next three examples reverse the hoop positions for Faith and Bob.

D. Faith's lead is 5, she should peg both balls out.

E. Faith's effective lead is 6, she should peg both balls out.

F. Faith's effective lead is 7, she should peg both balls out.

Tactics for one ball games.

1. You are in the lead

For most of the time when you are leading, just go for position in front of your hoop. Watch out for aggressive leaves by your opponent (see (2) below). If taking position is too dangerous, adopt the tactics that you would use if you were behind.

This may seem a very boring and negative approach, but in practice it isn't. Do not get lulled into a false sense of security when you have several hoops advantage. It only takes a good hit in by your opponent and your lead can soon vanish. In a friendly one-ball against Jill once, I gave her a six hoop advantage. I won by 1. The next game I lost by about 3.

Remember that the rules for a lift are unaltered. So if you use your opponent's ball and wire yourself from it, your opponent has a lift.

2. You are behind

The first thing you need to ask yourself is this, "Am I much better at running a hoop, then getting position for the next one in the continuation stroke than my opponent? If the answer is yes, are there enough hoops left for me to catch up by doing this?"

If the answer to either of the above questions is no, then somehow you have got to hit in. The tactics are very similar to the pegged out game.

● *Shoot — for a hoop or a ball.*

● *Lurk — near where your opponent has to go.*

● *Position — in front of the hoop that you want.*

Shoot.

This is the shot that you should take whenever you think that your chance of hitting is fair or better. Be on the lookout for giving yourself this chance. An example would be if you were for hoop 3 and your opponent had positioned for hoop 5. Running hoop 3 hard would take you close to your opponent. If you hit in, you will need to see if you can get a two ball break. If you cannot, then play a shot that will place yourself near (hopefully in front) of your hoop and your opponent some way from her/his. Concentrate more on position for yourself than too much on dispersing your opponent. Don't wire your opponent.

When shooting for a hoop from some distance back, i.e. you are not too sure about getting it, it is usually better to go softly. That way you stick in the jaws rather than bouncing away.

The most dangerous time for your opponent (and for you) is when you are running the middle hoops. It is impossible to position with any safety. Be ready for your opponent reaching these hoops so that you can plan to get near.

If you are only one hoop behind, try to arrange it so that you can run your hoop hard. That way you might catch up with your opponent waiting at the next hoop. Sometimes it is worth deliberately sticking in the jaws of your hoop to achieve this.

Remember that even if your opponent has just run rover and you are in front of penult, you still have a chance. This is because your opponent has to shoot hard at peg. If he/she misses you can get penult and lay up with a longish shot for rover which also attacks the peg. It's exciting stuff!

Chapter 2 had the saying "If your opponent will certainly finish next turn, shoot, otherwise join up." Modify this to "otherwise decide whether to shoot, lurk or take position."

Lurk.

The best places to lurk are either in corners or on the boundaries parallel to hoops. Any place just out of range will often do though. Choose a point where you think that a breakdown by your opponent is most likely. This will usually be the next hoop in order.

When should you lurk? When shooting is impossible or suicidal and taking position is pointless or suicidal. Remember that you do not actually have to hit a ball to take a shot. You can "deem" your ball as struck. It will remain it where it is. This can lead to the ridiculous situation where two players have crept up on either side of a hoop. They are now a foot apart but wired. Both players now refuse to move. In this situation call a referee who will adjudicate as best befits the circumstances.

Position.

This is the shot that you will play most often, even when behind. When positioning in front of a hoop to run it next turn, put yourself about a foot in front. Then you can run hard if you need to. This is very useful for hoops such as number 3. With the right strength you might get lucky and have a chance at hoop 4 with your continuation shot.

3. You are even.

I have been describing situations which will have occurred towards the end of a normal game. Occasionally one-ball games get used as a tie break for a tournament. I have played in one-ball situations on several occasions to decide a tournament. The most exciting was at the end of the 1986 Inter-Counties. Eastern Counties had to play 5 one-ball games to decide the winner. I lost my game but fortunately three others won theirs.

Many people say that if you win the toss you should go in second and I usually do. However if you lose, you can lay a tice near hoop 1. So I'm not sure there is much gain either way. The objective here, and in any other situation where you are even, is to get in front of the hoop. Not, however, in a position where your opponent can hit you, or at least, not easily. This can well mean several turns warily circling a hoop. Someone will crack and make the shot which spells either success or failure. If you get the success, remember that just one hoop ahead is a very vulnerable position.

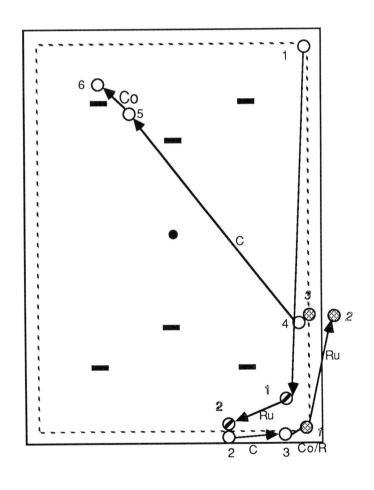

Fig 6.1   No break example.

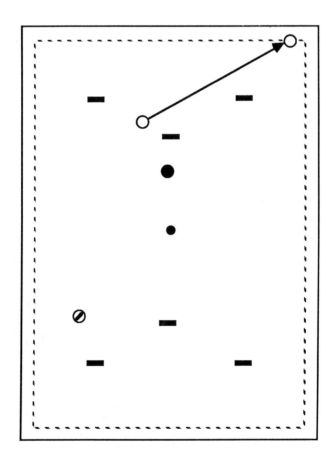

Fig 6.2   Defensive position having failed penult.

Chapter 7

Hampered Shots

*F*or a full definition on hampered shots, see the law book. Essentially a hampered shot is one where you are unable to make your normal swing. Additionally you may not be able to hit all of the ball with all of the mallet face.

I have said that this is a book on tactics rather than playing skills. Despite this, I am going to say just a little about playing hampered shots because of the psychology involved. A perfectly straightforward roquet of three feet suddenly becomes magnified into something horrendous. This has happened just because your backswing is slightly impeded and a referee is watching.

Always get a hampered shot watched if you are unsure about it and/or your opponent wants it watched. Similarly, have a referee watch hampered shots made by your opponent. You may ask a referee questions on the law, e.g. "What faults can I commit in this stroke?" You cannot ask for advice such as "How should I play this stroke?"

The law on faults.

This is the famous law 32. Ask a referee to explain and demonstrate it to you as soon as you have a basic grasp of the game. I am going to look at it in a slightly different light in that law 32 says what you must NOT do. I am going to concentrate on the unspoken what you CAN do.

Do not touch the mallet head with your hand or any other part of your body or clothing. You can therefore hold the shaft of the mallet as close to the head as you like. Just don't touch it. You can also hold the mallet in one hand, but the likelihood of this being of any benefit is small!

Do not put your arm, hand or mallet shaft on the ground or against your leg/foot. You can put any other part on the ground however. This means that you can kneel or squat so that you can get better position. You can also tilt your mallet sideways.

You must hit the ball with the face of the mallet. This means that if you hit the ball with ANY part of the face, it is a fair shot. The face does not include the bevelled edge (or just edge). By the way, an accidental hit with the bevelled edge is not a fault if your shot was not hampered.

Do not maintain contact, i.e. steer a ball or hit it twice in the same stroke. You can, however, swing your mallet in an arc provided that you then hit the ball cleanly. You can also double tap (but still not steer) when making a roquet or pegging out.

It is not legal to use your mallet to move or shake a ball which is near a hoop or the peg. It is legal to do so with another ball. Whether you move it legally or not, you are now responsible for its position, and may have given a lift.

Do not crush a ball against a hoop or the peg. You can however to an extent crush a ball from which you are taking croquet. Be careful though, you may well get penalised for something else, such as maintenance of contact.

Moveable and non moveable items.

You can move certain items if they get in your way. These are the clips, corner pegs and flags, filial on top of the peg and boundary boards. You cannot move hoops or the peg, without asking a referee first. This is true even when they are out of position. You may ask a referee if you can move a ball or balls if you have a problem with excessive damage to the lawn, eg a hole. It must be excessive, small depressions are the rub of the green. Although not law, it is common for two players to agree before starting a game, that damage to a particular corner spot is severe. They agree that players may move balls without asking. If you do move a ball you must move all other involved balls by the same amount. If that means moving a critical ball, you must call a referee anyway. After you have made this stroke and one more, replace any unmoved balls in their original positions.

Practice.

It is well worth while getting a referee to set up a series of hampered shots for you to make. He/she will show you clearly what are faults, and how to make many "impossible" shots without fault.

Chapter 8

Helpful Hints

*T*his chapter is a collection of snippets which will prove useful on the lawn. They are things that I have either worked out for myself or, more commonly, other people told me. This chapter then is a thank you to those who have helped me, in the hope that I can now help others.

I have starred the paragraphs as,

*   = Things which are suitable for all.
**   = Things which are suitable for people with handicaps less than 13.
***   = Things which are suitable for people with handicaps less than 9.

* If you are shooting badly, concentrate on hitting the ball cleanly and not on making the roquet.

* Do not be afraid to ask your opponent if you are not sure about something. This includes things that your opponent has done or might do. It may not be a problem, but you can ask. If you are still unhappy, call a referee. If you call a referee, remember the answer for future occasions. I would like to be able to say that all the opponents you meet will understand why you are asking. I regret that this is not true, there are a few irritable people about. If you meet them, don't let them upset you, just point out quietly that you are still learning. On the other side of the coin, do make sure that what you are asking seems sensible. If you need to ask something every 10 minutes throughout the game, then you ought not to be playing in tournaments yet.

* In a straight drive shot, your ball travels about a quarter of the distance of the other ball. The accuracy of position with your ball is therefore much more than in a take-off shot for short distances. This is particularly useful when approaching hoops.

*   Making a rush.

You must strike a balance when approaching for a rush. Get as close as possible to the rush ball because the closer you are the more accurate the rush. Unfortunately, if you try approaching too close, you could fail to get in the right position for a rush at all. You must decide for yourself which is the best compromise, based on your own abilities. For most players of handicap 6 and above, any rush more than a yard away stands little chance of going accurately. If you hit hard, there is a good chance of missing altogether.

To make a cut rush, work out where you have to strike the rush ball. Then step back and stalk from that direction. Figure 8.1 shows this. Get your aim, then forget the other ball and concentrate on making a clean stroke with the required strength. Do you find that no matter what you do you always seem to hit the rush ball almost dead centre every time? Then you are probably subconciously looking at the rush ball as you strike.

*   It is not an error for your ball to go off court after it has correctly run a hoop. Replace your ball on the yard line and take the continuation shot. This can be useful when you have a ball near the boundary behind your hoop. You simply have to run the hoop fairly hard without worrying about position for the subsequent roquet. If your ball crosses the yard line but does not go off court, do not replace it on the yard line. Take the continuation shot from where the ball lies.

*   Joining up with mother (your other ball).

You are completing a turn and intend laying up, perhaps with a rush to your next hoop. Try to do so that you do not give a double target to the opponent.

Avoid giving the "free" shot. This is a shot where your opponent can shoot at you and land safe if the ball misses.

If you can, lay up near a corner, but a few feet in. If your opponent shoots and misses, you can roquet the opponent's ball and send it forward as a pioneer. Or at least to somewhere useful, while at the same time getting a good rush for your next hoop.

The easy pioneers that you can get from corner positions are:

Corners 1 & 4. Hoops 4, 5, 6, 2 back, 3 back, penult, rover.

Corners 2 & 3. Hoops 2, 3, 5, 6, 1 back, 4 back, penult, rover.

In other words the north corners cover the north hoops, while the south corners cover the south hoops. All corners cover the middle.

If you cannot get to a corner, use a boundary which does not give a free shot.

Normally, do not lay up in the middle. This may mean giving up the innings. If your opponent is a good shot, or is close, this is the best thing to do. There are occasions where you can lay up in the middle. If the chances of hitting are slight and you give little away even if your opponent hits in, then join up. Do not however leave a double, even if to avoid doing so spoils your rush.

* Accuracy in croquet shots is much better if you can get a straight line, so plan your previous rush to achieve this.

* If you have a lift, you do not have to take it next turn. As long as you do not move the ball, you can take the lift at any time. Of course, in the mean time your opponent may well move it anyway!

** When you would have a lift shot but for your partner ball being clear, consider putting that partner ball into the A or B baulk. Make sure that this hides the partner ball. You will get a lift next time unless your opponent does something about it. You can of course, only do this if it is safe to leave the other ball there.

** Learn how to do jump shots once you have mastered all of the normal ones.

** There are two balls on the yard line, close together. You have roqueted one of them. Now you want to get a rush on the other, but the roqueted ball is in the way.

Do a little split shot. This will send the croqueted ball into the lawn and your ball into the yard line area for the rush.

The balls are very close and the previous shot is not possible or very difficult. Do a little half roll sending both balls into the yard line area, but don't send the croqueted ball off the court. Replace the croqueted ball on the yard line and take the rush.

131

Figures 8.2a and 8.2b illustrate these two moves.

** You are shooting for a ball on the boundary with the intention of taking a bisque if you miss. The likelihood of hitting is small. Consider deliberately missing on the side that gives you a good rush.

** When rushing a ball towards your hoop.

· The best rush position is about 18 inches to two feet in front of the hoop. Not quite in front but just off centre by an inch or two on the side that you wish to send the croqueted ball. This still applies if you want to send the ball directly behind the hoop but be off centre by about 6 inches.

If you can only rush to behind the hoop, put the rushed ball to where your take off approaches the hoop at about a 35 degree angle. This gives you more leeway if you make an error in strength on the take off stroke. See Figure 8.3.

If you land directly behind your hoop, do not try to approach it by going through the hoop backwards. Say you are a foot behind, see Figure 8.4. Aim just to miss the hoop upright, and get about 18 inches beyond the hoop. The angle of approach will still be reasonable.

If you land behind, but right up against an upright so that the approach is clear, do a little split shot approach. Figure 8.5 shows this. A take-off shot is liable to leave the croqueted ball impeding your path through the hoop.

If you land in the jaws of the hoop, you can take croquet from the correct side. The proviso is that your ball has not started to run its hoop. See Figure 8.6 for examples. Get a referee to judge this. If you are unable to take croquet from in front, you may be able to "Irish peel", ie send both balls backwards through the hoop. Then you run the hoop in the continuation stroke. There is a problem with this shot. Apart from the difficulty of getting it right, you may not be able to see the croqueted ball once you have run the hoop. It will help if you Irish peel with a normal drive rather than a roll. This will send the croqueted ball a couple of yards through the hoop and give a clearer path for running the hoop. With luck, you will also be able to make the return roquet having run the hoop.

*** You can "promote" one ball with another, without having to roquet it with your ball. Suppose that you have taken off to your opponent's balls which are together, but with one of them stuck in a hoop. You can roquet the free ball, rushing it just in front of the hoop. Then in the croquet stroke, knock the trapped ball free, hopefully getting a rush to your hoop. Of course this requires care and practice!

*** Cannon shots.

For the full law on cannons, see the law book, or ask a coach. The basic rule is as follows. You have just roqueted a ball and rushed it over the yard line. When replaced, it is in contact with another ball already on the yard line (or corner spot) You have a cannon. Take croquet from the ball that you have roqueted. Place the third ball against the croqueted ball, anywhere you like as long as it is not touching your ball. Figure 8.7 shows this.

I am going to describe just two out of the many types of cannon shot.

The first cannon shot is suitable for these situations :-

From corner.	Pioneer to.	Approaching.
1	2	1
2	2 Back	1 Back
3	4	3
4	4 Back	3 Back

Place your ball directly in line with the ball from which you are taking croquet, to send it as a pioneer. Then place the other ball at right angles to this line. Strike with a firm drive at an angle halfway between the straight line and your hoop. Figure 8.8 shows a cannon to 1 back and 2 back from corner 2.

A simpler shot is the bendy or banana cannon shown in Figure 8.9. This gives a rush but no pioneer. Place the three balls together (a). Give a little tap along the rush line. The middle ball will squeeze out, giving you a rush in the desired direction (b).

Many A class players scorn this cannon as error-prone and negative. I consider it suitable for high and middle bisquers because of its simplicity.

There is a variation on this, with a much exaggerated banana (c). Place both the ball that you intend to rush and your ball, directly along the rush line as before, but separated by only an eighth of an inch. Then place the croqueted ball so that it touches both the other two. Now treat the shot as a simple rush, ignoring the third ball. This variation, called a wafer cannon, is less prone to error in the rush. It is, however, more likely to send the croqueted ball off lawn when shooting from a corner.

There are many other cannon variations, some with 3 balls some with 4, but they are outside the scope of this book. The two that I have shown however work for most situations. They will at least enable you to do something constructive in a cannon situation. You will soon learn new ideas that will add to your repetoire.

Cannons need not be in a corner, they can be on the yard line. An example will be if you rush a ball directly behind another already on the yard line. True cannons cannot occur in court although balls will sometimes end up together in a similar configuration.

*** Peeling.

The best peeling stroke is the straight drive because it is the most accurate.

The ideal position is about 1 foot in front of the hoop. However, you may not want to run the same hoop with your ball. You will play the croquet stroke with a split, so a slightly angled approach may be better.

Line up the balls for a peel and decide on the type of stroke that you are playing. Concentrate on position for your ball and forget the peeled ball. This especially applies if you are intending to run the hoop with your ball in the continuation stroke.

If your shot is straight and you intend to run the hoop with your ball afterwards, it is normally better not to Irish peel. Run the hoop with your ball in the continuation stroke.

If your shot is not a straight one, remember that the ball that you want to peel will "pull." It will go towards the direction in which you are hitting. Pull is illustrated in Figure 8.10. The amount that a ball pulls will depend on the angle of shot. The more the angle, the more the pull up to about 35 degrees, then less again. It will also depend on the type of shot. Stop shots give the least pull. It will also vary with different balls and different weather conditions, and of course with the distance from the hoop. Typically, for a 35 degree, drive shot from a foot away, you will need to allow for about half an inch of pull.

Remember that in a croquet stroke you must not send either ball off court. There is the strange anomaly, however, that if your ball should run its hoop before going off that is alright. If the croqueted ball goes off, it is an error even if you have scored its hoop by peeling.

You can peel a ball just by hitting it through in a roquet stroke (a rush peel). Even knocking it through with another ball is a peel.

*** The law on hoop and roquet in the same turn is complex but essentially the situation is as follows.

NB. In this section, "The Ball" means the other ball which is in or just behind your hoop. You are correctly in front of your hoop with your ball. The shot that you are about to play is one where you intend to run the hoop. In all cases you hit The Ball (if you do not it is of course an ordinary hoop shot with a continuation stroke if you are succesful).

A.   The Ball is clear of the hoop on the non-playing side (behind your hoop as you look at it).

(i).   You have not run a hoop since roqueting The Ball.

If your ball has run the hoop when it stops moving, you score both hoop and roquet. Take croquet from The Ball. If your ball has not run the hoop, your turn ends.

(ii).   You have run a hoop since roqueting the ball or it is the first stroke of your turn.

If your ball has run the hoop when it stops moving, you score both hoop and roquet. Take croquet from The Ball. If your ball has not run the hoop, you score only a roquet. Take croquet from The Ball.

B. The ball is not clear of the hoop on the non-playing side, i.e. it is in the jaws.

(i). You have not run a hoop since roqueting the ball.

If your ball has run the hoop when it stops moving, you only score the hoop. You have a continuation stroke. If your ball has not run the hoop, your turn ends.

(ii). You have run a hoop since roqueting the ball or it is the first stroke of your turn.

You only score a roquet and you take croquet from The Ball.

***   Cross wiring.

The purpose of cross wiring is to leave both of your opponent's balls by your next hoop. Position them in such a way that they cannot see each other, i.e. you wire them. You then position your balls as far away as possible. Leave yourself a rush to the next hoop but one. Make sure that you leave each of your opponent's balls a clear shot for at least one of yours. If you do not you will give a lift.

A good example of cross wiring is at the end of a break where you have gone as far as you wish with your first ball. Cross wire your opponent at hoop 1 and lay up a rush to hoop 2 near corner 3. Figure 8.11 illustrates this.

If your opponent fails to hit in, you are always left with one ball still at your hoop. The disadvantage is that if you fail to get the wiring right you will leave your opponent an easy hit in.

The technique for good cross wiring rests on five main points.

i.   When you have run the last hoop before setting up the cross wire, you should already have your partner ball plus one other, near to the cross wiring hoop.

ii.   When running the last hoop, get a rush to the wiring hoop.

iii.   After wiring, your partner ball is the last used. You should get a rush on it to the corner that you have chosen.

iv.   When you take off for the rush on your partner ball, the ball from which you take off moves ALONG the wiring line. It should not move at right angles to it. That way having got a wiring, you do not lose it again.

v.   Arrange the cross wire diagonally across the hoop and at 1 — 2 yards from it.

Required direction of rush

Direction of strike

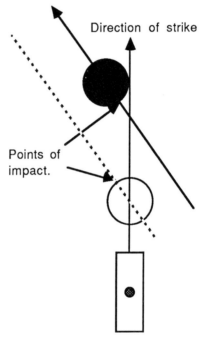

Points of
impact.

Fig 8.1   Working out the rush line.

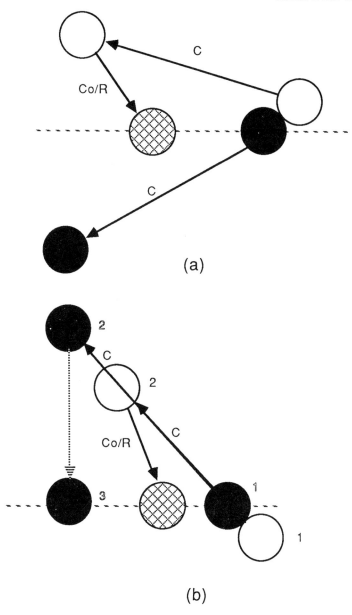

Fig 8.2   Getting a rush when two balls are close together.

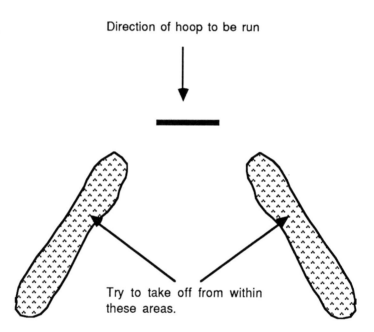

Fig 8.3   Take-off point when behind a hoop.

Direction of hoop to be run

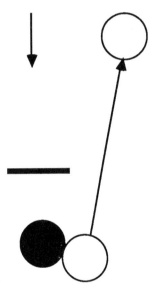

Fig 8.4   Approaching a hoop from directly behind it.

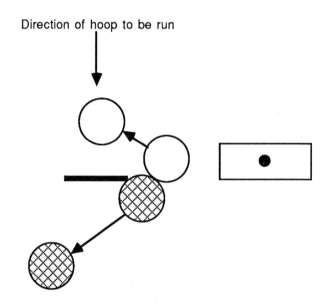

Direction of hoop to be run

Fig 8.5   Approaching a hoop when the roqueted ball is very near the hoop.

142

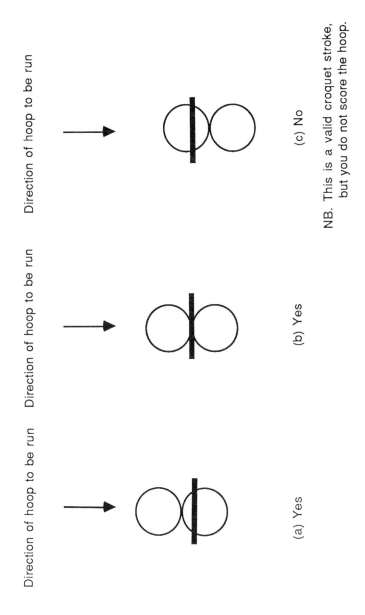

Fig 8.6   Positions where croquet can be taken to run the hoop.

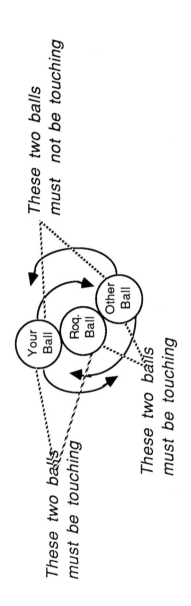

Fig 8.7 Ball positions for a cannon.

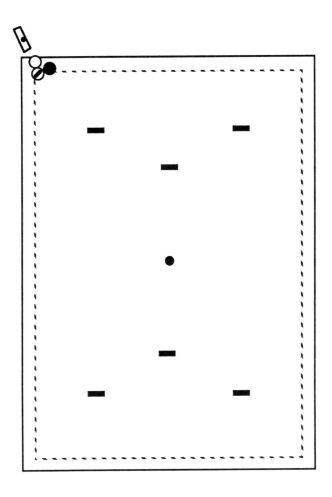

Fig 8.8   Corner cannon to 1 back and 2 back.

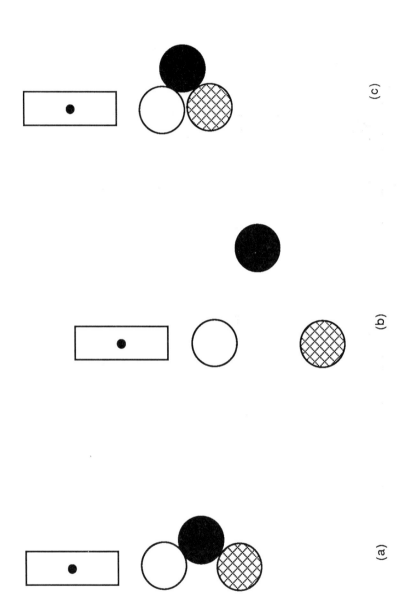

Fig 8.9   The banana cannon.

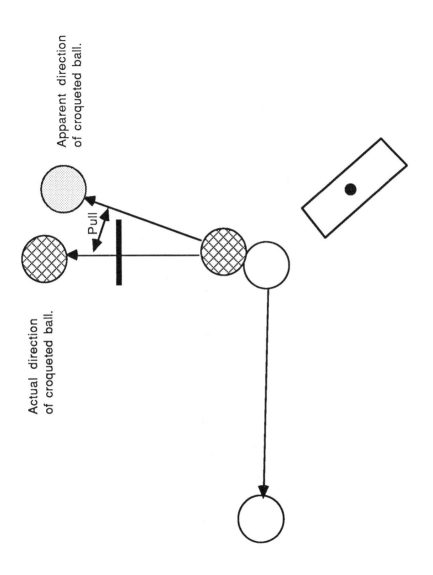

Fig 8.10   Pull.

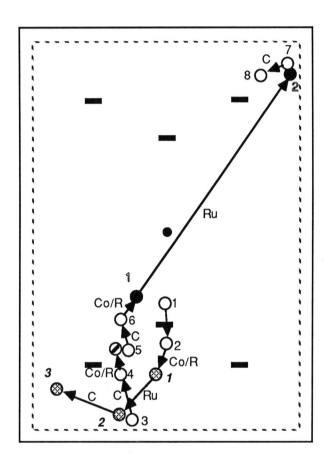

Fig 8.11   Cross wiring at hoop 1 (from just before running Rover).

Chapter 9

Other Types of Handicap Game

C hapters 1 to 8 considered normal handicap games. This one looks at some other variations that you will meet.

These are the variations I cover.

1. Doubles, where two pairs compete.

2. Full bisque games, where both players have all of their bisques.

3. Small Lawn Croquet, where play is on a half size lawn.

4. Shortened games, where you play less than 26 points.

In all of these variations, I will only write about the differences from standard croquet. Most of the time, your tactics will be the same.

Doubles.

Each player has one ball. One pair of players competes against the other pair. Pairs play alternate turns; however, either player of the pair can play at each turn.

Decide bisques as follows. Each pair adds their bisques together. Subtract the lowest from the highest. Take the difference, then round up to the nearest half bisque. The highest handicapped pair get this amount.

Examples.

Martin and Lewis are playing Nan and Edith. They play three games. For each game, Martin and Lewis have a different handicap.

Martin	Lewis	Total	Nan	Edith	Total	Difference	Halved	Rounded
1/2	3 1/2	4	8	12	20	16	8	8
1/2	2	2 1/2	8	12	20	17 1/2	8 3/4	9
− 1/2	4	3 1/2	8	12	20	16 1/2	8 1/4	8 1/2

Tactics

1. Try to have a captain of the pair.

Do not say " Oh well whoever is out there should play their own game." Together you should know your own strengths and weaknesses. Choose the better tactician as the captain. This is not necessarily the better player. There are many good singles players who are hopeless at doubles.

2. The non-playing partner should watch carefully.

An observer is nearly always in a better position to see the overall picture. Also, it is very easy to play the wrong ball in doubles. Do not leap on every few minutes however with trivial comments. See also the paragraphs on helping your partner and giving advice.

3. Do not have long mid-court discussions.

A doubles game almost always takes longer than a singles one. Discussions with your partner cause most delay. Players accept this, but make the discussions brief.

4. You can assist your partner.

You can place the ball for a croquet stroke. You can show what stroke to play and demonstrate the position in which to play it. You can stand at an aiming point while your partner lines up a shot. You can advise on hampered strokes. You should call a referee if needed.

You cannot play or demonstrate any actual stroke. You cannot stand at an aiming point while a stroke is being made. You should leave the lawn during actual play.

5. The number of peels is limited. You are only allowed four peels in total with your partner's ball. This does not include any peels made on opponent balls.

6. Use the bisques according to the situation.

If one player has a low handicap, one or two bisques can be very powerful. Use them as the need arises, not saved just for the high handicap player.

7. A low handicap player should not get too far ahead of a high handicap partner.

There are several reasons for this.

● It puts a psychological pressure on the high handicapped player.

● It increases the risk of the low handicapped player being pegged out.

● It reduces the chance of the low handicapped player being able to peg out the opposition.

In a timed game modify this rule. At about an hour before time, the low handicap player should establish a good lead on points. Do it this early because if left too late, the opposition will make things difficult. If you have the lead, you will do the same!

8. Have a basic game plan worked out.

8.1 Two high or medium handicap players are partners.

Play as in singles. Use any bisques to establish a break and go round, giving a leave for the other player at the end. With limited or no bisques, still use singles tactics. Do not worry about tactics 5, 6 or 7.

8.2   A high and a medium handicap player are competing

Play as in singles. Do not worry about tactic 6 or too much about tactic 7.

8.3   A low and a high or medium handicap player together.

a.   With bisques.

The low handicap player should set up a good leave for the partner, using a bisque if needed. If the opponents miss, the high/medium handicap player then goes round to peg.

b.   Without bisques.

Play as in singles, but rely on the better player to hit in and set up breaks.

c.   Giving bisques.

Let the better player hit in and set up tempter leaves to extract bisques. Try to get away from hoop 1 and lay rushes to hoop two. These have less danger from bisque taking.

8.4   Two low bisquers together.

This is outside the scope of the book.

Full bisque games.

Both players receive all of their bisques. So a handicap 6 has six bisques when playing a handicap 10, who has ten bisques.

If you are playing a minus player, you get the difference as in ordinary handicap croquet.

There are special rules for minus players in small lawn games, see next section.

Tactics.

There are only two situations where the tactics change from ordinary games. These occur at the start and at the end of a turn.

Always go in second if you can (modify this rule for small lawn games, see below).

When you finish a turn, remember that your opponent has bisques as well. Lay up with your opponent in or near two corners. Put yourself on the boundary, away from your opponent's hoops. Leave a wide join.

Small Lawn Croquet.

A small lawn is half the size of a standard one. The setting is the same. Only play the first six hoops and peg for each ball. This makes it a 14 point game. Games are full bisque, see previous section.

The rules are almost the same as standard croquet. The most important difference is in the wiring law. Wiring your opponent's balls gives a lift, even if your own are open.

Players below standard handicap 2 have to make 1 or more compulsory peels. There are a few rules associated with peeling. There is only one of real concern to you. If you peg out your opponent, you remove the obligation to do peels.

Calculate bisques according to this table (This is under review by the Croquet Association and may change).

Standard Handicap	Small Lawn	Standard Handicap	Small Lawn
6	2	12	6
6 1/2	2	13	7
7	3	14	7
7 1/2	3	15	8
8	4	16	8
9	4	17	9
10	5	18	9
11	6		

OTHER TYPES OF HANDICAP GAME

Tactics

1. Do not worry about being pegged out.

Even an indifferent hitter can usually hit in on a small lawn. If you have bisques, you can set up a three ball break. If you don't, you can usually get several hoops on a two ball break.

2. Play aggressively.

One of the major purposes of small lawn games is that they provide spectator interest. A small lawn tournament has been televised. Everything is designed to provide a quick, exciting game. Defensive play is usually a waste of time, but occasionally you will have no choice. When this happens you just have to do the best you can and hope that the short shot gets missed.

Players with small lawn handicaps above 4, should ignore the paragraph above when playing each other. You can still make defensive leaves with some confidence.

3. Consider going round on turn 3.

If you get a lucky hit in and/or you are playing well, it is worth going round on turn 3. That way your opponent can only follow you to peg and perhaps peg you out. You are then just left with a second all round three ball to finish.

Shortened games.

Because of the complicated calculations involved, the rule book contains a list of bisque calculations for shortened games.

The 22 point game.

All clips start on hoop 3. Be careful, remember to go to hoop 5 after hoop 4. It is easy to forget your starting point and go from hoop 4 to hoop 1.

_154_

The 18 point game.

There are four variations but only two are common.

i.   All clips start on hoop 5. Starting is tricky if you are giving bisques or playing without them. Unless you have a good rush and a guaranteed hoop, don't try. Take off to the hoop or lay up a rush for next time whichever seems best. I do not like this start. It gives the receiver of bisques the advantage of three easy hoops to get going. Your only defence is to make things as difficult as possible.

ii.   All clips start on hoop 1.

As soon as a ball runs hoop 1, the partner clip is put on 3 back. This is a fairer variation. It also gives the A class player a chance at something called a quadruple peel. Here, as well as running the 12 hoops with one ball, the second ball is peeled through its 4 hoops. It doesn't happen very often, usually there is a breakdown. The other player then gets an easy break. However, as Celia knows, it can be done. I think that she has forgiven me!

The 14 point game.

Only run the first six hoops with each ball, then peg. This is an unlikely variation in a serious tournament, but you might get it at club level. Do not confuse this with small lawn croquet. That has a different size lawn and rules.

OTHER TYPES OF HANDICAP GAME

Chapter 10

Thank you for the Game!

Congratulations! The game is over and you have won. Are there any customs to observe? The answer is yes, and to round of this book, I will describe what they are.

Thank your opponent for the game. Your opponent should also thank you in turn, but don't expect the same enthusiasm as you have! Some players like to shake hands as well.

Note the score. Your opponent's score is deducted from yours and you win by that amount.

Example 1. You have pegged out (scored 26 points) and your opponent has scored 18 points. You have won by $+8$.

Example 2. You have scored 17 points and your opponent has scored 12 points, after time. You have won by $+5$ on time.

After you have noted the score, check that your opponent agrees. Then clear the lawn of clips and balls.

Report your score to the manager and find out when you are required to play next. If there is a gap before your next game, do not leave the club without asking the manager first.

It is usual, but not mandatory, to offer your losing opponent a drink. It is not always done, so watch what others do.

It remains only for me to wish you luck in your games. If you play me at some time in the future and beat me $+26$, tell me that it was all due to my book! It will make defeat easier to bear!

Don Gaunt
Ipswich
1987